Columbia

PACIFIC OCEAN

Washington

Vancouver Island

Jervis Inlet

Toba Inlet

Bute Inlet

Loughborough Inlet

Knight Inlet

Kingcome Inlet

Drury Inlet

Seymour Inlet

Rivers Inlet

Queen Charlotte Strait

Johnstone Strait

Howe Sound

Strait of Georgia

Juan de Fuca Strait

Vancouver

Sandheads

Brockton Point

Point Atkinson

Porlier Pass

Active Pass

Portlock Point

Saturna Island

Discovery Island

Merry Island

Trial Islands

Fisgard Island

Victoria

Race Rocks

Sheringham Point

Ballenas Islands

Sisters Islets

Entrance Island

Chrome Island

Chatham Point

Cape Mudge

Carmanah Point

Pachena Point

Cape Beale

Amphitrite Point

Lennard Island

Pulteney Point

Scarlett Point

Pine Island

Nootka

Estevan Point

Cape Scott

Quatsino

Triangle Island

enbroke land

N E S W

LEGEND

☼ STAFFED STATION

◇ UNSTAFFED STATION

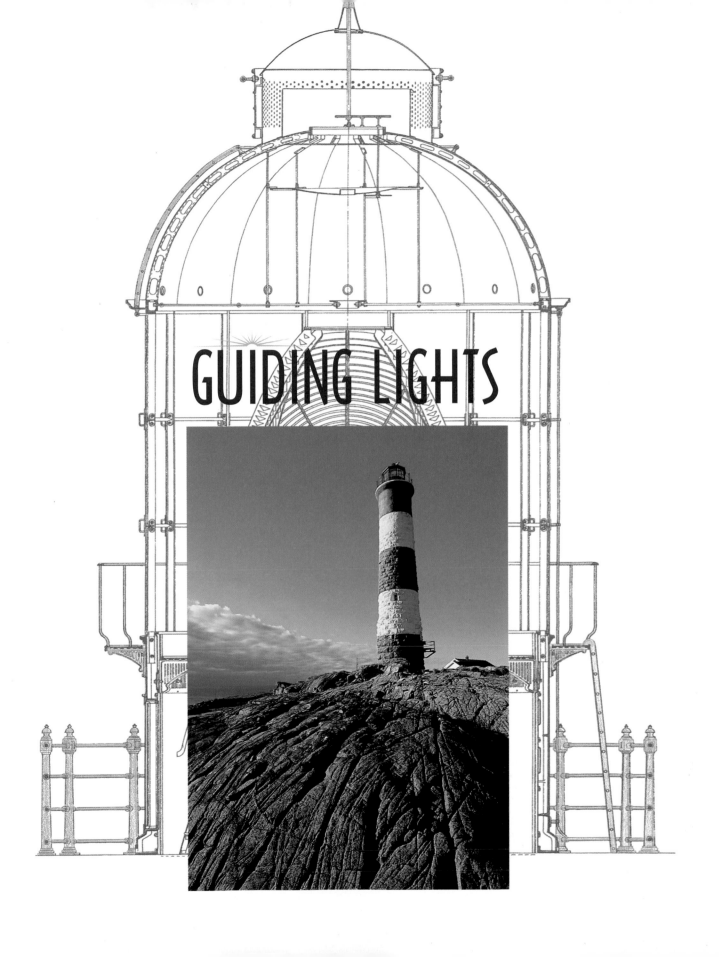

GUIDING LIGHTS

GUIDING LIGHTS

British Columbia's Lighthouses and Their Keepers

Text by Lynn Tanod
Photography by Chris Jaksa

Harbour Publishing

The powerful light on one of the rocky Sisters Islets off the southwestern shore of Lasqueti Island in the Strait of Georgia has a range of 21 nautical miles. The station, erected in 1898, provides a bearing between Hornby and Lasqueti Islands and warns of the presence of the low-lying Sisters.

Previous pages: Established in 1891, Carmanah Point lighthouse sits on the southwest coast of Vancouver Island, marking the entrance to Juan de Fuca Strait. The light shines 55.6 metres above the waters known as the "Graveyard of the Pacific."

6
On the Lights

10
Part One:
City Lights

32
Part Two:
Graveyard of the Pacific

62
Part Three:
Northern Lights

88
Part Four:
Beacons of the Inside Passage

111
Looking Back

On the Lights

Keeper Iain Colquhoun looks out from the lens he describes as "a masterpiece of optical engineering." The First Order Fresnel lens at Pachena Point lighthouse is one of only two that exist in British Columbia, and it has now been mothballed.

IT ALL STARTED WITH A HEADLINE. "TAKE A PICTURE. THEY'RE ALL SOON GOING TO BE UNMANNED," THE VANCOUVER SUN *DECLARED ON JANUARY 14, 1995.*

For British Columbia's lightkeepers, it was the next round of a decades-long fight to keep lightstations staffed. For photographer Chris Jaksa and me, it was the beginning of a journey that led us to some of the most remote regions of the province and introduced us to the unique people who operate one of the most extensive networks of staffed lighthouses remaining in the world.

Chris and I had always been attracted to lighthouses in the same way that most people are, whether they've seen one or not. I grew up in landlocked Ottawa, so the only lighthouse I ever saw was the tower relocated from Cape North, Nova Scotia, to the lawn of the capital's Museum of Science and Technology. The closest Chris came to a lighthouse was the short fibreglass beacon on a pier from which he and his father fished in Lake Ontario. It wasn't until we moved out west that we encountered the real thing. At Point Atkinson, we met Donald Graham, the keeper who retraced the turbulent history of his predecessors in his books *Keepers of the Light* and *Lights of the Inside Passage.*

Lightkeeping began on the West Coast in 1859 when George Davies stepped off the boat from England to tend Fisgard light. Fisgard was the first of 59 lighthouses erected over the next 100 years along the BC coast. Although lights were established on the East Coast as early as 1733, it wasn't until the shipping boom of the late 19th century that the federal government decided more lighthouses were needed in the West. By that time, hundreds of lives had already been lost to the 27,200 kilometres of unmarked coastline.

Life was not easy for early lightkeepers like Davies. With no assistance, no escape in times of crisis, and no emergency communications, keepers were sometimes reduced to flying their flag upside down in the hope of being seen by a passing vessel. Others were forced to make perilous trips in their own small rowboats, more than once perishing in view of their horrified families. More often, however, it was passing mariners who had the emergencies and the keepers who had to make dangerous, sometimes heroic, efforts to save them.

Chris and I were intrigued. Graham's books opened up the rich past, but we wanted more. We wanted to see the towering lighthouses designed by engineering genius Colonel William Anderson. We wanted to witness the wave-swept wilderness that wrecked so many ships and both crushed and inspired so many keepers. But mostly we wanted to meet the people who choose this career for themselves today. Who are they? What do they do? Why do they do it? We decided to hit the road.

As we soon learned, there are few roads to hit. Even today the majority of British Columbia's staffed lighthouses are accessible only by boat, by aircraft or on foot. And though technology has eased the burden of isolation, life on the lights can still be trying. The conveniences that most people take for granted are unavailable at many lighthouses. Supplies are delivered by helicopter or ship once a month; if keepers run out of milk, the nearest corner store is a long way away. Private chats with "townfolk" are impossible since most stations don't have regular telephone service. All calls must be directed through a Coast Guard radio operator who, along with anyone else who has a scanner, can hear the entire conversation. At times even flushing the toilet is a luxury. When the station's cistern of rainwater gets low come summertime, every drop needs to be conserved.

Despite the inconveniences, many keepers cherish their isolation. They *want* to be alone. As they often told us, there is a big difference between being alone and being lonely. "On the lights, the first person you meet in isolation is yourself," explained one 38-year veteran, "and you better like the company."

Most lightkeepers find great satisfaction in the job itself. Operating the equipment and maintaining the station fixtures are among the obvious duties, but one of the keepers' less recognized tasks is providing accurate weather reports. Day and night, keepers relay detailed observations about the sea and sky conditions in their area for the Coast Guard's continuous marine radio broadcast. Because weather can vary greatly within just a few kilometres, the lightkeepers' information is vital to pilots and mariners planning their routes along the coast.

Often ravaged by Pacific storms in the winter, Ivory Island lightstation was established in 1898 to act as a landfall for vessels in Milbanke Sound and to guide them through islands off the BC coast. Located 14 miles northwest of Bella Bella off Robb Point, the southwest extremity of Surf Islet, the light was devastated by massive waves in 1904, 1963 and 1982.

Lightkeeping has never been limited to these regular duties, however. Keepers also collect environmental data for scientists, offer mariners advice over the radio, assist boaters with engine trouble, and participate in rescues. They are often the first to spot boats in trouble. Armed with their radios, binoculars and intimate local knowledge, keepers notice immediately when something is amiss in their piece of the ocean.

Nevertheless, the Canadian government has worked for three decades to bring the tradition of staffed lighthouses in British Columbia to an end. User groups as diverse as the Coastal Communities Network, the Sea Kayak Association of British Columbia and the BC Aviation Council challenged the policy. They argued that the new technology designed to replace lightkeepers would cost more than retaining them and wouldn't be as reliable. Even people who had never used the services of a lightstation felt strongly about the issue. The philosophy of replacing humans with machines offended some, while others pointed out that automation often resulted in the destruction of historically significant buildings.

Despite the controversy, the Coast Guard automated Discovery, Ballenas, Point Atkinson, Sisters, Active Pass, Saturna, Porlier Pass and Race Rocks lightstations in 1996 and 1997. But in a surprise announcement on March 28, 1998, David Anderson, the federal Minister of Fisheries and Oceans, announced that the keepers at the rest of British Columbia's staffed lights would stay. However, their future is far from secure. At some stations, the automation equipment remains, towers are slated for removal and keepers wait anxiously to see how long this latest decision will last.

Guiding Lights is a tribute to the great tradition of staffed lighthouses on the BC coast. It is a portrait of the people who continue, despite all odds, to keep that tradition alive.

Opposite: Strategically placed in 1885 at the north-eastern entrance to the channel that separates Galiano and Mayne Islands in the Strait of Georgia and familiar to generations of BC ferry travellers, Active Pass lightstation warns mariners of the treacherous Georgina Shoals northeast of the light and serves as a guide through one of the busiest shipping routes between Vancouver and Victoria.

Keepers can play an important role during emergency situations by cooperating with search-and-rescue crews. Here, a Coast Guard auxiliary unit practises night manoeuvres off Trial Islands lightstation.

PART ONE

City
Lights

S helter from the storm. Safe haven. Sanctuary. Down through the ages, the glint of the lighthouse has always been a welcome sight to beleaguered mariners returning to port. Pharos, the first known lighthouse of the Ancient World, invited ships into Alexandria with a great fire that blazed atop a 90-metre tower. Indeed, most of the world's oldest lighthouses were established to guide ships into city harbours.

North America's first lighthouse was built in 1716 to guard the approach into Boston Harbour. In Canada, the lights marking the entrances to Halifax on Sambro Island (1758) and to Toronto on Gibraltar Point (1808) are among some of the country's oldest city lights. The first towers in British Columbia, Fisgard and Race Rocks, helped guide ships into Victoria. They, along with Victoria's Trial Islands and Vancouver's Point Atkinson and Brockton Point, were the West Coast's original city lights. To seafarers, their illumination heralded journey's end. To many of us today, these towers still speak of security and home.

Above: Sitting astride the southern entrance to the Inside Passage, Discovery Island lies at the junction of Haro and Juan de Fuca Straits. The lightstation, seen here with Greater Victoria in the background, was established in 1886 and warns mariners of dangerous tidal streams and submerged rocks in the vicinity.

Opposite: Stanley Park's Brockton Point lighthouse was an opportunity for marine engineer Colonel William Anderson to show off his architectural finesse to the public. In 1914 Anderson rebuilt the tower, supporting it with arches under which admiring pedestrians could stroll.

Every morning keepers at Entrance Island, and those at every other lightstation on the West Coast, wake up at 3:30 a.m. to file their marine weathers. The reports describe sky and sea conditions, visibility, precipitation, and the speed, direction and character of wind. Their accurate, timely, 360-degree observations of the specific conditions in their area allow mariners to plan ahead and prepare for upcoming changes in the weather.

Located in the Strait of Georgia, Entrance Island lightstation marks the northern approach to Nanaimo Harbour. Because of its close proximity to the city, there is a high volume of pleasure boaters and kayakers in the area. In 1995, *Wave-Length*, a BC paddling magazine, organized a demonstration in support of keepers in which more than 100 kayakers formed a "human life preserver" around the island.

Fisgard Island

THE FADED HANDWRITING IN THE JOURNAL ENTRY HANGING ON THE DOOR OF THE FISGARD LIGHTHOUSE RECORDS THE MOMENT THE TRADITION OF LIGHTKEEPING BEGAN ON CANADA'S WEST COAST:

> *Friday Nov. 16th. Commence Lighting. 1st watch G and R Davies 1/2 past 4 till 8 Oclock.*
>
> *2nd watch G Davies 8 Till 12 Oclock. alls well. 3rd watch R Davies 12 till 4 Oclock alls well.*
>
> *4th watch G Davies 4 till 8 Oclock. alls well. Length 16 hours. weather fair. Sign. G. Davies.*

When George Davies lit the lamp in the tower on that autumn afternoon in 1860, a light shone out for the first time from British Columbia's original lighthouse. Reading his words more than a century later, I wonder what that day was like for Davies and his wife, Rosina. Did the couple's three children climb up the spiral staircase with them to witness the first lighting in the lantern room? Did the wick catch the flame on the first try? Did the crews of the ships anchored in Esquimalt Harbour ring their bells or let out a cheer when they first saw Fisgard's beam shining 21 metres above the water?

Inside the restored lighthouse is a list of lightkeepers' duties developed in England in the early 1800s. They include such edicts as "The Lightkeepers shall keep a regular and constant watch in the Light-room throughout the night" and "The Lightkeepers are required to be sober and industrious, cleanly in their persons and linens, and orderly in their families." From November 16 onward, Davies and his family followed a similar routine to that described by him in the lighthouse's daily journal. As they tended the light, observed the weather and watched the movements of vessels coming in and out of the harbour, could they have possibly imagined that 138 years later their home would be a national historic site and their words read by 48,000 visitors a year?

Fisgard was established after Captain George Richards completed a safe-harbours survey of the coast for Her Majesty's ships and recommended installing a light on Fisgard Island to guide vessels into the rapidly growing centre of Victoria. Because Fisgard was an "imperial" light, the cost of its materials and construction was assumed by Great Britain. The lightkeeper, the lens and the lantern apparatus arrived from London, England, after a 196-day voyage on the *Grecian*. Tinted glass was also sent to be used in the windows in the lantern room, though many of the ruby shades shattered while rolling around in the hold of the ship. After Davies supervised the installation of the apparatus and the lantern, the light in the Fisgard

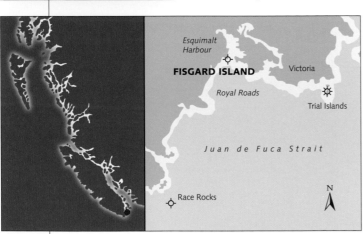

Above: Fisgard lightstation's combined dwelling and tower looks much the same today as it did when the light was first established in 1860 to guide vessels into Esquimalt Harbour. Of British Columbia's city lights, Fisgard is the only one that has been preserved in its original state.

tower flashed red, green and white. In his 1861 navigational guidebook, *Vancouver Island Pilot*, Richards described how the colours were to be used by mariners headed for Esquimalt Harbour:

The white light is intended to guide a vessel in from seaward and while visible clears the western coast between Race Island and Esquimalt ... the red shade will be found useful by vessels bound from the eastward ... a W.S.W. course will lead a safe distance from Brotchie ledge, until the light changes from red to white.... The green shade is to avoid the Whale rock in the upper part of the harbour.

Although the last keeper left Fisgard in 1928, the automated light still guides a steady flow of traffic into the harbour. The week Chris and I visit, the HMCS *Regina* is anchored in port. Several of its crew have come to the museum, one of whom noted in the guest book that visiting the lighthouse "feels like home." The comment suggests what is so special about Fisgard lighthouse. It feels familiar to everyone: experienced mariners, occasional boaters or landlubbers like us. The island setting, the red brick house with shuttered windows, and the spiral staircase up the tapered white stone tower all conform to our romantic idea of what a lighthouse should be. Fisgard is the lighthouse of our memories and our imaginations.

Between 1860 and 1928, 12 different keepers climbed up and down the 51 steps of Fisgard's famed wrought-iron staircase. While one keeper stayed on the small island for as long as 19 years, another withstood the isolation for only 12 days.

Top: Each year 48,000 tourists visit Fisgard lighthouse. The light is one of the most photographed attractions in Victoria.

Bottom: For the past 20 years, Fisgard volunteer tour guide Pen Brown has also played the part of Santa Claus. The 74-year-old grandfather brings cheer to lighthouse kids all over the south coast each holiday season via Coast Guard helicopter. A former keeper himself, Brown hopes his visits make Christmastime "a little less lonely, a little more enchanting."

The lives of Fisgard's early keepers were often disturbed by gunshots. When soldiers at nearby Fort Rodd Hill practised firing their artillery, keepers were warned to lock up the shutters around the lantern to prevent the glass from breaking.

Race Rocks

"HOLD ON!" YELLS OUR CAPTAIN HENRY CANCADE AS A WAVE SLAMS INTO OUR 4.8-METRE FIBREGLASS BOAT. "IT'S ROCK-AND-ROLL TIME!" MOVING DEFTLY OVER THE SWELLS, HE GUIDES US OUT OF THE SHELTERED WATERS OF PEDDER BAY INTO JUAN DE FUCA STRAIT.

Spray-soaked and white-knuckled, Chris and I exchange worried looks as we head toward the Race Rocks lighthouse. The winds howl around us and sea lion bulls as big as station wagons lunge in our wake. Glancing at the threatening clouds beyond the black-and-white striped tower, I am glad that we radioed keeper Mike Slater before we left; he will be watching out for our arrival.

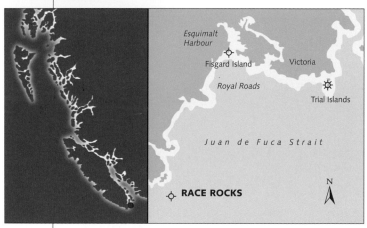

Built at the same time as Fisgard, the imperial light on Great Race Rock was first lit on Boxing Day in 1860. The light serves as a marker for vessels approaching Esquimalt and Victoria Harbours and as a warning to mariners attempting to round the cluster of small, rocky islets. As early as 1846, Captain Kellet of the survey vessel HMS *Herald* noted the need for a light at Race Rocks, writing that "This dangerous group is appropriately named for the tide makes a perfect race around it."

More than a century later, the waters are no less hazardous. Chaotic seas often result when wind-driven waves counter the current; heavy riptides can easily grip a vessel and drag it onto the rocks at a rate of up to seven knots. Mike Slater, who has been on the lights for more than 30 years, has personally pulled in a dozen people from the unruly sea. "My rule is: have a healthy respect for the old lady," he tells us when Henry drops us off, relieved, at the dock. "These currents are nobody's friend. They can sink anything and anyone."

Above: At Race Rocks, Lester B. Pearson International College students lead an educational tour for a group of sixth-graders. The station's tower, a recognized historic building, was constructed with precut and numbered Scottish granite blocks shipped overseas as ballast by the British Admiralty in 1860.

Mike and his wife, Carol, have been at Race Rocks for nine years. A roll-up-the-sleeves, hands-in-the-grease, let's-get-down-to-business kind of guy, Mike always has a project on the go. His latest involves rigging up a pipe system that pumps salt water to an aquarium in the old boathouse. Students from nearby Lester B. Pearson International College come to the island to study specimens of the area's unique marine life.

When I ask the Slaters about the rescues, Carol explains, "We're not going to look outside our window and watch someone drown. We just did it as a matter of course. But," she adds, "we're not going to wave a flag around and say, 'Hey, look what we did!'"

One thing they did was save the lives of two people they spotted on a foggy November evening. Mike and his partner, Gerry Toner, had been looking outside for the cat when they saw a quick flash off North Rock. It was the flashlight of two fishermen whose boat had hit a deadhead and was sinking fast. Both were hypothermic from being in the water and their hands were like hamburger from shooting off flares. By the time the keepers reached them, the two men had almost lost hope.

Over the years, Mike has hauled many others into his Boston Whaler and brought them to safety, including two teenage kayakers who found themselves flailing in 3.5-metre swells, a family in a sailboat that got caught up on North Rock, and two teenagers in an open aluminum boat with nothing but their life jackets and a bailing bucket.

Recently Mike was recognized for his 33 years as an employee with the Canadian Coast Guard. A framed certificate thanking him for his loyal service "on behalf of the government and the people of Canada" lies casually on an end table. Mike doesn't give it much thought. It doesn't really compare to the phone conversation he had one December morning. "You never know how you can get a lump in your throat," he recalls, "until you get a call from someone on Christmas Day, thanking you for saving her husband's life."

Following pages:

Washington State's Olympic Mountains and a fogbank are the backdrop for the 24.4-metre-high tower on Great Race Rock. The light cautions mariners approaching the dangerous riptides and back eddies that swirl around the islands.

Race Rocks Marine Ecological Reserve

Mike Slater awaits a group of divers from Lester B. Pearson International College. In 1980 the staff and students of the college successfully lobbied the government to protect the area as a marine ecological reserve. When the station was automated in March 1996, the college also came to a unique agreement with the Coast Guard whereby the lightkeepers would remain at the site as guardians of the reserve. Mike and Carol Slater are now employed by the college to deter poachers, record environmental infractions and generally provide a coast-watching presence.

Seasonally Race Rocks is inhabited by a roaring mob of up to 1000 Steller's and California sea lions. The waters around the lightstation are a transition zone between the open ocean and inner coastal waters. They are swept constantly by strong currents that supply rich nutrients for innumerable underwater organisms. Pearson College students come to the island to study the diverse marine life and to give educational tours to local elementary school children.

Trial Islands

BY THE TIME KEEPER IAIN COLQUHOUN ARRIVED IN THE STATION BOAT, KAYAKER JAMES WEITMAN'S FINGERS WERE TOO NUMB TO TIE A ROPE AND HE WAS SHIVERING SO MUCH HE COULD BARELY TALK.

He and his friend Jeff Beitz had just abandoned their latest plan to get to safety and were trying to keep up their spirits by joking about "Plan F." Their predicament was hardly funny. Twenty-seven-knot winds were whipping across Juan de Fuca Strait, two-metre seas were battering their kayaks, and James was in the water, his half-submerged boat as useless as his out-of-reach life jacket. What had started out as a minor mishap when a wave threw James out of his kayak had rapidly escalated into a life-threatening situation. Night was falling, and the tide was pulling them both farther out into the strait.

"We were thinking, What next, what next?" James tells me. He had been in the water for almost 20 minutes and was wearing only the bottom half of a wetsuit. "The waves just kept coming and coming. They were relentless. I remember seeing the lighthouse on the island and thinking, I sure hope that's not already automated."

It wasn't. Trial Islands light, established in 1906, is the last Victoria-area lighthouse to remain staffed. Heavy riptides off Staines Point and strong tidal streams that occasionally reach six knots can make the waters around Trial especially dangerous to smaller craft like kayaks.

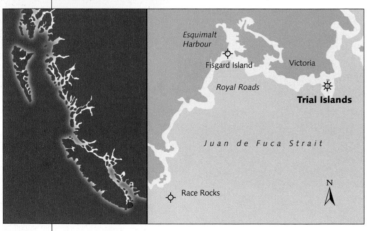

Above: Randy Turner, coxswain of the Victoria Coast Guard Auxiliary's fast-response vessel, checks out the landing possibilities at Trial Islands station. He, along with 1200 additional volunteers on the coast, is a crucial part of British Columbia's search-and-rescue network.

Assistant keeper Kathy Doyle had been drinking a cup of tea when she noticed a kayak floating backward approximately half a nautical mile due south of the island. When she picked up her binoculars for a closer look, she determined that there were actually two kayakers and one was in the water. Immediately the rescue plan was put into action:

21:15–Vancouver Coast Guard Radio and Rescue Coordination Centre are notified.
21:19–Keeper Iain Colquhoun heads out in the station boat. High seas and spray limit Iain's visibility so Kathy directs him by radio.
21:25–Iain arrives on the scene and helps James into the station boat. A Canadian Coast Guard Auxiliary rescue boat and the CCG Narwhal 1 also arrive.
22:00–The Narwhal 1 tows back the kayak. The auxiliary takes James back to Oak Bay after he dries off and warms up at the lightstation.

James tells me that it wasn't until he was safe inside with Kathy and Iain, wrapped in a blanket, that the severity of the situation sank in. "I realized, Oh, my God! I don't know if there were guardian angels out there or what, but I sure am thankful."

James told his story to the media and participated in the Coast Guard's public consultations on lighthouse destaffing. But not everyone helped by keepers is so outspoken. James thinks there are probably quite a few people who, after avoiding injury or even death through the actions of a lightkeeper, convince themselves that they were never *really* in any danger. "We never forgive those who make us blush," someone once said; most keepers never again hear from the people they help.

Before the Trial Islands lightstation was established in 1906 off Oak Bay, ships leaving Esquimalt Harbour would do a "trial" run to the islands and back before heading on their way. Today the light warns mariners of the unpredictable riptides in the area and aids them as they enter Haro Strait from Juan de Fuca Strait or as they travel through Rosario Strait and Admiralty Inlet.

Brockton Point

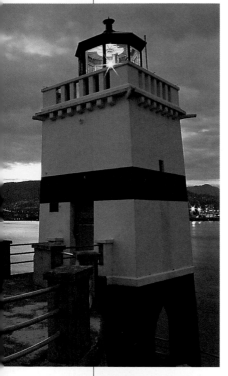

IN THE SHADOWED FOREST BEHIND VANCOUVER'S BROCKTON POINT LIGHTHOUSE, HIDDEN FROM THE VIEW OF THE FAMILY PLAYING ON THE BEACH AND IGNORED BY THE ROLLERBLADERS WHO WHIZ BY ON THE STANLEY PARK SEAWALL, IS A MONUMENT DEDICATED TO THE VICTIMS OF THE CHEHALIS TRAGEDY.

Engraved on the granite cross are the names of the eight people who perished when the tugboat was smashed to pieces by a steamer in 1906. The wreck of the *Chehalis* happened right off Brockton Point in full view of the lighthouse's first and only keeper, Captain W.D. Jones.

By the time the lighthouse was established in 1902, Vancouver had become a major port. Two new sawmills and the completed railway line contributed to the increase in shipping traffic. With so many vessels leaving and arriving, there were numerous opportunities for collisions. The combination of heavy volume and human error accounts for the more than 100 wrecks, including the *Chehalis*, that are rotting on the harbour's bottom today.

On July 21, 1906, Jones was sitting outside the lighthouse watching the approach of the fastest and most glamorous steamer on the coast—the 91-metre-long, 1814-tonne *Princess Victoria*. Dozens of people had gathered at the light's lookout to admire the "white flyer" and wave to its 200 passengers. Just ahead of the *Victoria* was the 18-metre-long, single-propeller tugboat *Chehalis*. Both vessels were bucking a heavy flood tide in the First Narrows as they headed around Brockton Point. As the steamer gained on the tug, Captain Griffin of the *Victoria* ordered two whistles blown to indicate that he was going to pass on the *Chehalis*'s port side.

It must have been a horrifying moment: a sunny day, a peaceful cruise along the city shore and then pandemonium. The steamer was doing 20 knots when it hit the tug amidships and sent its occupants flying into the water. Eight of the 15 people aboard died, including a young boy and a newlywed couple. Some were sucked down into the whirlpool created by the sinking tug, while others narrowly escaped being sliced apart by the propeller of the oncoming *Victoria*. One survivor owed his life to a quick-thinking woman who threw him a life ring from the steamer, and another was saved when a deckhand tossed him an orange crate. The engineer of the *Chehalis* was rescued by Jones, who rowed out to the scene as soon as the steamer hit the tug.

West Vancouver

Point Atkinson

Burrard Inlet

Brockton Point

English Bay

Point Grey

Vancouver

N

Above: Stanley Park's Brockton Point lighthouse in Vancouver marks the abrupt turn into Coal Harbour for inbound vessels and guides outbound marine traffic toward First Narrows.

Opposite: At dawn two sentinels guard Burrard Inlet: Elek Imredy's *Girl in a Wetsuit* and Brockton Point lighthouse.

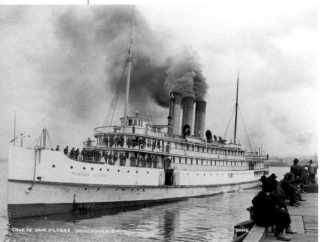

It was neither the first accident off Brockton Point nor the first rescue by Jones. During his 25-year career, he saved 16 people from drowning and was awarded a gold medal for his services. The "gallant captain," as Jones was known by the press, was also a graceful host whose homemade blackberry wine and intricate 3.6-metre flower sundial were known throughout the city.

When Jones retired in 1925, his home was torn down and his gardens paved over for a parking lot. However, the place from which 70 people witnessed the *Chehalis* accident is still one of the best spots in the city from which to watch the marine traffic of one of the busiest ports in North America.

As the sun goes down, I stop under the arches of the lighthouse and watch the lights flicker and the boats head for home. The Nine O'Clock Gun, fired by the "gallant captain" every day for 25 years, still rumbles in the distance.

Previous pages: Although Brockton Point's light has a range of 11 nautical miles, here it has to compete with the brilliance of the North Vancouver night skyline.

Top: On July 21, 1906, the passenger steamer *Princess Victoria* was involved in a tragic collision with a tugboat off Brockton Point, resulting in the deaths of eight people.

Bottom: Many people, including newlyweds Angela and Jason Lee, use Brockton Point's fabulous location as a backdrop for wedding photographs.

Point Atkinson

ON THE GLOOMY AFTERNOON OF SEPTEMBER 18, 1994, A PLAQUE WAS UNVEILED AT POINT ATKINSON LIGHTHOUSE IN WEST VANCOUVER TO COMMEMORATE ITS DESIGNATION AS A NATIONAL HISTORIC SITE.

The foghorn, fondly known throughout the surrounding metropolitan area as "Old Wahoo," wailed its baritone lament throughout the ceremony, drowning out the speeches of the politicians.

The Point Atkinson foghorn was a sound familiar both to those on the waters of Burrard Inlet and those in the communities around the lighthouse. In fact, the air-chime horns that replaced Point Atkinson's original diaphone horn replicated the sound of one of Vancouver's oldest and most significant auditory artifacts. Researchers with the World Soundscape Project, an aural-awareness program founded by Canadian composer Murray Schafer, described the foghorn as an integral part of Vancouver's acoustic environment. The first time I ever heard the horn's deep bellow, I felt oddly comforted. However, for Point Atkinson's earliest lightkeepers, the foghorn was the bane of their existence.

When a wooden tower was first erected in 1875 to mark the entrance to Burrard Inlet, a captain requiring the horn to navigate in the fog would alert the keeper with two blasts of his ship's whistle. The keeper then went outside and pumped a twin-bellowed horn by hand. But by the time the concrete tower that stands today was constructed

in 1912, the technology of fog signals had transformed the life of the lightkeeper. With the development of the steam-pressured horn, the keeper became responsible for sounding the horn whenever there was fog.

Today only the odd technician tends to the horn at Point Atkinson. In 1996, less than two years after Point Atkinson's national historic site plaque was presented, Old Wahoo was silenced forever when the Coast Guard replaced the horns with a short-range electronic high-pitched whistle and delivered a pink slip to lightkeeper and author Donald Graham. The two events typified the perilous fate facing British Columbia's lighthouses and their keepers.

Above: The Point Atkinson lighthouse in West Vancouver guides mariners in and out of First Narrows and Vancouver Harbour and cautions them about the strong riptides caused by the meeting of tidal streams from Burrard Inlet and Howe Sound.

POINT ATKINSON

New high-pitched 835-hertz foghorns now replace the bullfrog bass of Atkinson's famous "Old Wahoo," a move historian Donald Graham says "cut the vocal chords of Vancouver."

Above and left: Visitors to West Vancouver's Lighthouse Park enjoy kayaking, sunsets and fine stands of old-growth Douglas fir. The 75 hectares of virgin forest were spared from the axe because the federal Department of Marine and Fisheries of yesteryear required a dark backdrop for the lighthouse.

PART TWO

Graveyard
of the
Pacific

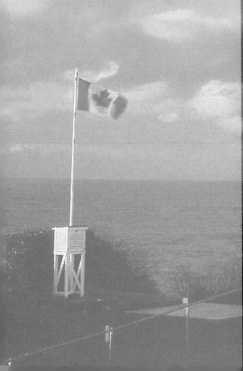

*C*oloma, Michigan, Uzbekistan, Janet Cowan, Sarah, Lillie, Laura Pike, Erikson, Pass of Melfort, Valencia...The full roll call of ships wrecked in the Pacific Graveyard will never be confirmed. Nor is the death toll calculable. What is known is that the waters off Vancouver Island's west coast are some of the most treacherous in North America.

Until Cape Beale, Pachena and Carmanah lighthouses were built, the coast-line between Barkley Sound and Port San Juan was shrouded in darkness. Rough seas in the winter, fog in the summer and the deceptive Davidson Current made navigation extremely dangerous for mariners heading for Juan de Fuca Strait. Ships often overshot the northern entrance to the strait and ended up instead on the rocks and reefs of Vancouver Island. The warning call of "Breakers ahead!" was always unexpected and usually too late.

Above: Amphitrite Point lightstation marks the entrance to Ucluelet Harbour and provides a landfall for mariners on the central-west coast of Vancouver Island. The station was established in 1915, but the distinctive bunkerlike tower wasn't completed until three years later.

Opposite: Because of its formidable 44-metre-high site and the lack of nearby sand, Pachena Point lighthouse couldn't be built with concrete. Today the station, located on the world-famous West Coast Trail, is the coast's last remaining wooden tower.

Following pages: Situated amid the beauty of Clayoquot Sound near Tofino, Lennard Island lightstation marks a landfall for vessels on the west coast of Vancouver Island and warns of dangerous reefs in the area.

33

Sheringham Point

SPREAD ACROSS THE BRUTON FAMILY'S KITCHEN TABLE ARE SCORES OF PHOTOGRAPHS, NEWSPAPER CLIPPINGS, LETTERS AND MAGAZINE ARTICLES THAT DOCUMENT THEIR LOVE OF LIGHTHOUSES.

There is a faded photograph of keeper Jim Bruton inside the lantern room at Sheringham Point lighthouse, an interview with his daughter Elanie about growing up at a lighthouse, a piece about a B-movie that was filmed at the lightstation, and countless shots of the tower.

Jim Bruton was the lightkeeper at Sheringham Point from 1968 until the station was automated in 1989. His four children spent much of their childhood on the lights. Today Elanie, 42, and Sharon, 40, share with me a lifetime's worth of lighthouse collectibles, ranging from glass floats found on the west coast of Vancouver Island to jigsaw puzzles of Sheringham's tower. The two sisters are true lighthouse aficionados, as is Sharon's husband, Ed Kerrigan. Their enthusiasm for the lights culminated almost 25 years ago when the couple were married in the lantern room of the Sheringham Point tower. Before heading out to revisit the site of the wedding, they tell me a little bit about the long history of their lighthouse.

Halfway between Carmanah Point and Race Rocks, Sheringham sits on a rocky point that juts into Juan de Fuca Strait. The point was named in 1846 in honour of Vice Admiral William Louis Sheringham, the British commander who helped Sir Francis Beaufort develop the international wind-force scale. Until the Sheringham station was established in 1912, the strait was marked only by lights at Carmanah and Race Rocks. In between the two were 48 nautical miles of darkness. When fog further blinded mariners in the strait, there were often shipwrecks.

The *Ann Bernard* was one such wreck. The barque went down on a grey February evening in 1862 while en route from San Francisco to Sooke. When the vessel encountered thick fog, Captain Olmstead and his seven-man crew could hear the surf but could see nothing until they struck rock several miles from Sheringham Point. As the vessel quickly broke apart, the captain jumped into the ocean to try to swim to shore. He made it safely, but two others drowned after their lifeboat flipped. Shocked, the rest of the crew climbed up the rigging and

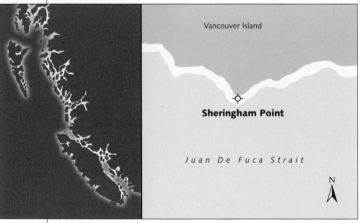

Vancouver Island

Sheringham Point

Juan De Fuca Strait

N

Above: Who says lighthouses aren't romantic? Sharon and Ed Kerrigan hope to return to Sheringham Point to renew the vows they made almost 25 years ago in the lantern room of the lighthouse.
Opposite: Surrounded by surging surf, Sheringham's slender tower rises almost 20 metres.

hung there in the damp cold. Hours later, low tide allowed them to wade to shore and join their captain in safety.

During the Brutons' time at Sheringham, there were no wrecks and very few accidents. In fact, Sharon and Elanie have only fond recollections of their time there. Their best memory of lighthouse life, though, was Sharon and Ed's wedding day. "This place looked a lot different then," says Ed, shaking his head at the forlorn appearance of the station when we arrive. A barbed-wire fence surrounds the overgrown grounds and there is only a patch of gravel where the Brutons' childhood home once stood. "On that day, this was the most beautiful place in the world."

On December 4, 1976, the station's red and white railings were adorned with flowers and the houses were abuzz with excited guests. Sharon and her bridesmaids carried their bouquets and lifted their ankle-length skirts as they climbed the ladders to the top of the tower. Sixteen people, including the minister, gathered for the ceremony in the lantern room, the interior of which was painted bright blue for the occasion. Over the crash of the ocean, Sharon and Ed broadcast their vows on CB radio to the delight of their guests below and their friends in the United States. Perhaps their "I do's" brought a smile to the faces of fishermen scanning their radios out on the strait.

Visitors to Sheringham's destaffed lighthouse are greeted with a two-metre-high barbed-wire fence and a No Trespassing sign.

Carmanah Point

WHEN THE CARMANAH POINT LIGHTHOUSE WAS FIRST ESTABLISHED IN 1891,

ONLY A FEW UNLUCKY SHIPWRECK VICTIMS WERE LIKELY TO VISIT IT.

The West Coast Lifesaving Trail, built in the spring of 1907 in response to the hundreds of wrecks along the west coast of Vancouver Island, led survivors of marine disasters through the rainforest to the warmth and safety of the lightstation.

Today more than 8000 people per year pass through the station while hiking what is now known worldwide as the West Coast Trail. Many of those who set out on the 77-kilometre trail from Pachena Bay to Port San Juan are unprepared. During the summer months, principal keeper Jerry Etzkorn and his family regularly give assistance to hikers, be it a glass of water and some encouraging words or a bandage for a twisted ankle and a call for an emergency helicopter medevac.

The day we visit, a chopper is at the station, but there haven't been any accidents. It's moving day at Carmanah. Assistant keepers Kip and Sandra Hedley are leaving their home of eight years to relocate to a lighthouse farther north on Scarlett Point in the Inside Passage. "It will be sad to leave this place," says their 10-year-old son Blair. "I won't be seeing Crusty, Plucky or Seldom Seen ever again."

Crusty is a rooster, Plucky, his devoted hen, and Seldom Seen, a fort that's hidden in a tree overlooking the station. From his leafy retreat, Blair watches the action as his parents and the Etzkorns prepare the sling loads.

Moving from a lighthouse isn't just a matter of hiring someone to pack boxes into the back of a truck. The Hedleys' possessions are secured in nets as big as parachutes. Once attached to the longline, the sling loads dangle 33 metres beneath a helicopter as the pilot swings them over the ocean and drops them onto the deck of an awaiting Coast Guard ship. The task is difficult: one wrong move and the family's belongings will tumble into the sea.

"It's a delicate process," says Jerry. "People are still finding silver balls washing up on the shore from when a box of Christmas ornaments fell in the ocean five years ago."

After the sling loads are safely deposited on the CCGS *Bartlett*, Blair takes a last look at his treehouse and heads down to the water with his parents. As the workboat nears shore,

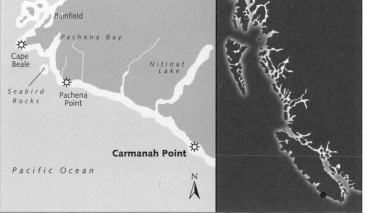

Above: Keeper Jerry Etzkorn enjoys the view from the lantern room of the Carmanah Point tower. From here he can see the Cape Flattery lighthouse on the Olympic Peninsula in Washington State. Together the two lights mark the northern entrance to Juan de Fuca Strait.

Bamfield
Pachena Bay
Cape Beale
Nitinat Lake
Seabird Rocks
Pachena Point
Carmanah Point
Pacific Ocean
N

Blair looks anxious. This will be his first overnight trip on a ship. "But," he says with a wary smile, "I'm not nervous." As the crew cautiously nudges the workboat's bow against the rocks, they yell for the Hedleys to jump in quickly. Blair looks back up at the lighthouse. "Goodbye," he calls with a wave. "Goodbye."

Far left: Over the years, Carmanah keepers have helped a variety of people enjoy the incredible coastline in Pacific Rim National Park, including hypothermic hikers, wetsuit-clad surfers, a cougar-attack survivor and even a spooked man who crawled out of his tent to discover a dead body on the beach.

Left: Jake Etzkorn helps with a move. Promotions, a desire to be near family, and cabin fever are all reasons for moving. Tension between the family of the principal keeper and that of the assistant keeper may also prompt relocation. "When you throw a bunch of strangers together in such close quarters," explained one keeper, "people can find themselves getting incensed over something as trivial as a tomato plant."

Below: A sturdy fibreglass workboat transports the Hedley family to a waiting Coast Guard ship that will take them to a new posting. British Columbia is one of the last places in the world where open surfboats are still used to supply lighthouses.

Following pages: Justine Etzkorn sometimes uses the feathers of her pet rooster, Crusty, to make flies for fishing. His mate provides the family with a constant supply of fresh eggs.

Pachena Point

STOPPING HALFWAY UP TO THE LANTERN ROOM OF THE PACHENA POINT LIGHTHOUSE, I TAKE A DEEP BREATH. IN THE CEDAR SCENT IS THE SMELL OF HISTORY. THIS OLD TOWER HAS WITHSTOOD THE BATTERING OF ALMOST 100 YEARS' WORTH OF RAIN, SEA SPRAY, SLEET AND SNOW.

Built in the wake of the *Valencia* tragedy, the Pachena station has warned mariners of the perils of the Pacific since 1907. Keeper Iain Colquhoun, Chris and I are on our way to the top of the last remaining wooden lighthouse in British Columbia. It is the only one to have survived the elements and humanity's desire to put up concrete.

Thirty-one steps below me is the octagonal base that once doubled as a dance floor and a classroom. When the lighthouse was established, so, too, was a marine radio station. By 1910 a small community of keepers, radio operators and their families lived on the grounds. They used the tower as a meeting place and a schoolhouse. You can still see the dusty bookshelves neatly tucked in against the massive support beams of the tower.

Today Pachena Point has a population of two. The floorboards of the tower haven't seen dancing for quite some time. Instead they are the home of a cedar-strip canoe and dinghy, handmade by Iain with driftwood. From somewhere above me, I hear his distinctly Scottish voice telling Chris that Pachena's First Order Fresnel lens was featured in the 1908 edition of *Encyclopaedia Britannica*.

Above: Pachena Point's historic wooden tower and First Order Fresnel lens, since shut down in favour of a plastic "bulb on a stick."

The dioptric lens sent over from England and meticulously pieced together on-site was considered to be at the cutting edge of navigational-aids technology.

"It really is a work of art," says Iain as I step into the lantern room. It's true. The lens looks like a giant glass beehive, its crystal prisms tinged gold from years of reflecting light from an oil-wick lamp. It is more than twice my 1.6-metre height, and it would take at least six people to join their hands in a circle around it. Each of the four flash panels has a double bull's-eye of convex glass in its centre that is in turn surrounded by concentric rings of glass. Inside the lantern room, the heat can be intense; after a half hour, we are all flushed with a rosy glow.

At the turn of the century, the keeper spent hours up here, cleaning oil residue from the massive lens and straining off the mercury on which it floated. Every three hours he climbed the tower to rewind the clockwork mechanism that kept the lens turning. Since the 1920s, the light source and movement of the lens have been powered by electricity. The mercury, though, has remained. It acts as a frictionless support bearing; Iain can move the two-and-a-half-tonne lens with just his baby finger. While old-time keepers continually handled the potentially dangerous substance in order to maintain the light, Iain has never come into contact with it. Two recent Health Canada tests confirm that the levels of mercury vapour are within safety guidelines.

The Fresnel lens itself has yet to be improved upon. It is the ultimate combination of science and aesthetics. Using the optical principles of refraction, reflection and polarization, the lens enables a 1000-watt bulb to send out a four-million-candlepower beam. The light is so bright that the only limit to its range is the curvature of the Earth. Rare throughout the world, Pachena's double bull's-eye lens is the only one of its type on the West Coast.

Later that night I am awakened by rattling windows and crashes that shake the whole house. When I look outside, I see the flag whipping furiously in 45-knot winds. Beyond is the absolute darkness of the sea. Then Pachena's radiance lances through the night. As the lens revolves, the four twin bull's-eyes illuminate the billions of moisture particles in the air, sending out what look like eight laser beams moving across the sky.

I wonder what it would be like to be out there in a gale like this, alone in the wheelhouse of a small fishing boat, peering through a spray-soaked window and hearing the wind whistling through the masts and rigging. Seeing the Pachena light would surely be a comfort. Even to the crews of those deep-sea freighters miles offshore and loaded to the gills with every conceivable navigational gadget, the light must be a welcome sight.

It was with sadness we heard a few months after our visit that the Coast Guard had ordered Pachena's great beacon sealed away behind a curtain and replaced by a much dimmer lamp on a 4-metre pole outside the tower.

In 1908 Gertrude Richardson came to stay at Pachena lighthouse to keep her bachelor brother company. The isolation was more than she could bear. One morning she jumped to her death on the jagged rocks below the station.

Left: Keeper Iain Colquhoun stands on the catwalk in front of Pachena's powerful Fresnel lens. When the light was lit for the first time on May 21, 1906, it was visible 35 miles away. Now it gathers dust.

Below: Fifty-two handmade signs in languages from around the world welcome hikers on the West Coast Trail.

A wave-battered boiler is all that remains of another victim of the Pacific Graveyard: the 630-tonne steam schooner *Michigan*.

The Valencia Tragedy

On the night of January 20, 1906, Captain Oscar Marcus Johnson made a fatal mistake. As he navigated the 76-metre passenger steamer *Valencia* through the fog looking for Juan de Fuca Strait, he neglected to account for the current. Turning toward what he thought was the mouth of the strait, he ordered a full stop when a large dark object was seen ahead. It was too late. As the ship struck the rocks near Pachena Point, Johnson bellowed into the night, "In the name of God, where are we?"

Although the people on the ship could see the shore, waves and reefs prevented them from reaching it alive. And though they were tied high in the rigging for protection, not one woman or child survived. One hundred and seventeen people perished in the horrific three-day ordeal, one of the worst disasters in West Coast marine history. The tragedy forced the federal government to begin construction of both the Pachena lighthouse and the West Coast Lifesaving Trail.

Cape Beale

AT CAPE BEALE THE WIND ECHOES THE GHOSTLY WAILS OF THE

SHIPWRECKED MARINERS LOST TO THE "GRAVEYARD OF THE PACIFIC."

The air outside is heavy with salt and moisture, and below the cliff where I stand with keeper Norbie Brand, the waters sound restless.

High above an ocean floor littered with hundreds of wrecks, the Cape Beale lighthouse marks the entrance to Barkley Sound. Built in 1874, it was the first light to be established on the treacherous west coast of Vancouver Island. Despite over a century of technological advancement, wrecks still happen off the cape. No one is more aware of that fact than Norbie, a 20-year veteran of lightkeeping. Today the former navy lieutenant with the lilting German accent invites Chris and me to see the evidence of the sea's destructive power for ourselves.

After a good hour of strategic bushwhacking and rock clambering, however, we finally give up. Norbie figures he's misjudged the location, and Chris is getting anxious about the incoming tide, so it comes as a complete shock when we scramble around the headland and see it. Hanging upside down, five metres above the water and wedged into the rocks, is the wreck of the *Dalewood Provider*. The aluminum hull of the 15-metre fishing trawler glitters in the late-afternoon sun. Shards of twisted metal dangle from the stern, and a frayed rope sways in the breeze. We have found the wreck. Norbie closes his eyes and lowers his head. "I feel like I'm seeing it again for the first time," he says.

The *Dalewood Provider* was wrecked when a storm blew in unexpectedly, late on the night of December 9, 1995. Norbie's block-lettered notes in the logbook of the Cape Beale lightstation methodically record the events of the days that followed:

Dec 10

1241—SPOT OVERTURNED ALUMINUM VESSEL IN FRONT OF CAPE BEALE

    —INFORM TOFINO

    —TOFINO INFORMS ME NO VESSEL IS OVERDUE

1400—SPOT TWO FLARES IN MUD BAY AREA

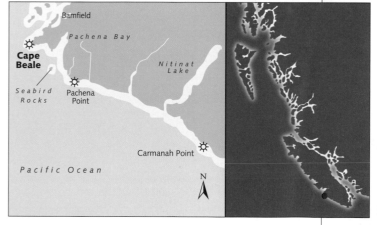

Above: Cape Beale's lighthouse was the first to go up on the shipwreck-prone west coast of Vancouver Island. Originally it was thought the cape would be the focus of major development in the area, but grandiose plans came to naught.

Above: Dozens of vessels have been wrecked in the Pacific Graveyard during keeper Norbie Brand's two decades on the lights. "Out here," he says pensively, "it's live by the sea, die by the sea."

Below: We Stand on Guard for Thee: the Canadian flag flaps beside Cape Beale's 9.7-metre-high lighthouse. The distinctive tower is targeted for removal by the Coast Guard.

Opposite left: The view from atop the landbridge that leads to the tip of Cape Beale is impressive. The ocean surges beneath the 20-metre-high archway over which Norbie crawled during the *Dalewood Provider* incident.

Opposite right: Norbie contemplates an archival photo of the wreck of the *Coloma*. He stands a mere kilometre away from where, almost a century ago, the ship's crew was saved from certain death by Minnie Patterson.

Following pages: More than 50 metres above sea level, the red and white lights of Cape Beale mark the entrance to Barkley Sound. The station acts as a landfall light for trans-Pacific shipping, guides vessels along the coast and warns mariners of offshore reefs.

—2 AMERICAN COAST GUARD HELOS IN AREA
1430—AMERICAN HELO PICKS UP SURVIVOR
    —OTHER CREW MEMBER DEAD
    —THIRD CREW MEMBER MISSING
1600-1930—SEARCH CAPE BEALE HEADLAND FOR MISSING CREW MEMBER
    —NOTHING
Dec 11
0919—AMERICAN HELO SPOTS MISSING CREW IN DEADMAN'S COVE
    —RETRIEVED—DECEASED

Norbie's memories of the incident are still vivid. He remembers the gales were so strong that December afternoon that he had to crawl on his hands and knees to reach the tip of the cape. He remembers the smell of diesel in the surf and the sound of metal scraping against rock. And he remembers hearing on the radio the next morning that the man whose name he had called out for hours during the previous night's search was dead.

"Nothing seemed real that day," Norbie says, his voice cracking. "Especially the sky. The sky was surreal. It was wild and moody and crazy and dark, but then the sun dared to come out. It was like someone up there was mocking us."

It is difficult for Norbie and his wife, Kathi, to talk about the *Dalewood Provider*. They wish there was something more they could have done. I wonder aloud if there would have been a survivor at all if rescuers hadn't known to focus their search around the Cape Beale headlands. The boat had not been expected back in Bamfield for several more days and there was no record of a Mayday. Had Norbie not seen it, nobody would have known that a wreck had occurred.

In response Norbie looks at the darkening sky. "The sea, she doesn't care, but we do. We have eyes and we're watching." He scans the horizon and counts out the lights of one, two, three boats on the water. "We can't say that we'll stop the boats going down. This big ocean has taken people in the past and she will in the future. But if we can prevent an accident, or save one life, it's worth it. We've done our job."

Minnie Patterson: Canadian Hero

On December 7, 1906, after a night of 80-knot gales, Cape Beale lightkeeper Tom Patterson awoke to a horrific sight. A sinking barque, the 51-metre *Coloma*, was drifting straight toward the rocks of the cape, its crew of 10 clinging desperately to the broken mizzen mast. With no boat or life-saving equipment at the station, the only hope of rescuing the sailors was by alerting the steamer *Quadra* in nearby Bamfield Inlet, but the storm had taken down the telegraph lines. Bamfield could be reached by a rough trail, but Patterson couldn't leave his post, so his wife, Minnie, set out on the gruelling nine-kilometre hike. She hitched her skirts and waded waist-deep through the freezing water of the lagoon behind the lighthouse, crawled through salal, and slogged through mud. At times she had to grip the fallen telegraph wire to keep her way in the rain and hail. Four hours later, the drenched and exhausted woman made it to Bamfield and got the *Quadra* away. Everyone aboard the *Coloma* was rescued, and Minnie Patterson's place in lighthouse lore was established.

1909

Estevan Point

IT TOOK 30 METRES OF REINFORCED CONCRETE, SIX FLYING BUTTRESSES, THE SWEAT OFF THE BROWS AND BACKS OF TWO DOZEN MEN, AND THE GRAND VISION OF MARINE ENGINEER COLONEL WILLIAM PATRICK ANDERSON TO CREATE THE MOST DRAMATIC TOWER IN BRITISH COLUMBIA.

Estevan Point lighthouse reaches into the sky like a rocket poised for takeoff. Its design is as unique and modern today as when it was built in 1909.

It's hard to imagine the actual construction of the tower in such an isolated place, but the faded photographs in the Estevan lighthouse scrapbook suggest the hardship endured by the work gangs. There was no road through the tangled rainforest and no safe boat landing. When part of the eight kilometres of track they had laid down for a horse-drawn tramway was washed away by high tides and a storm, the men pushed the cement and gravel to the site themselves with wheelbarrows.

"It just goes to show you how tough the old boys were at the turn of the century," says principal lightkeeper Dave Edgington. "There's not many men left today who would have the guts to build that thing out in the middle of nowhere." Dave explains that Estevan's flying buttresses were designed to help brace the tower against heavy winds. If you stand in the lantern room during a good storm, you can actually feel the tower swaying, he warns us before Chris and I begin to ascend the spiral staircase.

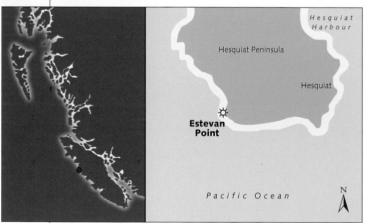

My thighs are burning and I feel a little dizzy, but the climb up the 155 stairs is worth it. The view from the top of the West Coast's tallest lighthouse is literally breathtaking. From the red-railed catwalk, I look out at what some mariners describe as the most challenging passage on Vancouver Island's west coast. Below me, boulders deposited by receding glaciers sit atop a striated rock shelf that stretches underwater for a couple of miles. Cirrus clouds streak the sky and a light breeze blows from the southeast. High above the shore, a large nest is visible in the snag of a decaying tree. I can't see the eagles who live there, but I can hear their distinctive skittering calls.

If I were religious, I might feel inspired to pray. Instead, I sing. I try a few tentative arpeggios inside the lantern room and then get a bit bolder with a tune from Mozart's *The Marriage of Figaro*. The flying buttresses of the tower are reminiscent of Europe's grand cathedrals, and

Above: After 15 years on the lights, Estevan Point keeper Dave Edgington wouldn't live anywhere else. "People say keepers are all nuts," he admits, "but that's what we say about people who choose to live in the city."

Map labels:
Hesquiat Harbour
Hesquiat Peninsula
Hesquiat
Estevan Point
Pacific Ocean
N

so are the acoustics. Musicians have lugged their instruments up the stairs to play a private concert for Mother Nature and to hear their music bounce off the walls. My voice warmed up, I give in on my way down and belt out a totally inappropriate camp song. When I reach the bottom floor, Chris, in his best Captain Highliner voice, recites the poem given to us by the lightkeeper:

The angry coast, the rocky reefs,
No more are feared by man
And those that sail, will never fail
To praise the light of Estevan.

The last word said, we look up and listen as the echo of Chris's voice reverberates throughout the tower.

Above: Estevan's federal-government designation as a classified heritage building can be partly attributed to its flying buttresses. The inward cant of the buttresses on the tapered 30-metre-high octagonal tower creates the illusion of even greater height and substance, prompting Frederick Talbot to declare Estevan "the last word in lighthouse building" in his 1913 book, *Lightships and Lighthouses*.

Left: Not for those with vertigo: visiting Coast Guard ship crews have a running wager on the fastest ascent of the 155 steps up Estevan's spiral staircase.

ESTEVAN POINT

On June 20, 1942, at 9:25 p.m., Estevan lighthouse was purportedly shelled by the Japanese, an act that increased wartime anxiety among Canadians and prompted Prime Minister Mackenzie King's government to push forward with conscription legislation. However, some allege that the attack came not from a Japanese submarine but from an American or Canadian cruiser in an effort to secure Canada's commitment to the war effort.

Following pages: Located on the tip of Hesquiat Peninsula, the West Coast's tallest lighthouse is a visual essay in support of Francis Bacon's maxim that "Art is man added to nature."

Hobbies: Keeping Busy On the Lights

The lightkeeper who whittles away the hours making model boats may seem a romantic myth, but in the case of Estevan keeper Dave Edgington, it is true. Dave thinks that model-making taught him a patience he didn't have when he first came on the lights. "I swore I was going to take a hammer to that more than once," he says, pointing to the finished stern-wheel paddler now displayed in a glass box on the wall. While Dave builds, his wife, Louise, knits or sometimes makes *chilkat*, a hand-spun wool woven with cedar bark that is used in the ceremonial dress of some First Nations peoples. She markets her work along with the crafts of a dozen other lightkeepers in a computer-generated gift catalogue.

Nootka

"HAVE YOU MET PAT AND ED KIDDER YET? THEY'RE QUITE THE CHARACTERS" IS A COMMON REFRAIN AMONG LIGHTKEEPERS, RADIO OPERATORS, PILOTS AND MARINERS ALL ALONG THE BC COAST.

The Kidders are described to us as "a couple of radicals," "the best friends you could find on a stormy night," "the barnacles on the rock" and "legends in their own time." The couple have earned their reputation by living on the lights the longest, rescuing the most people and being particularly vocal against the Coast Guard's automation plans.

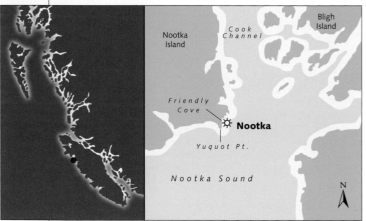

Above: Keeper Ed Kidder has used his 4.2-metre rigid-hull inflatable Hurricane 400 to bring gas to mariners, tow their boats, search for them when they are missing and, sometimes, save their lives.

Nootka light is the Kidders' seventh lighthouse. Established on San Rafael Island in 1911, the station marks the entrance to Nootka Sound and overlooks Friendly Cove. Inside the church at the cove, photographs, documents and artwork combine to tell the stories of early contact between the Native peoples and the Europeans during the late 18th century. On March 30, 1778, Captain James Cook became the first white man to set foot on the land that Maquinna, leader of the Mowachaht, called Yuquot, "place of winds."

Ed and Pat's long lighthouse history began when they were high school sweethearts in Nanaimo. Pat's father decided to become a keeper and moved the family to nearby Entrance Island. "I thought I was at the end of the world," she says. "Me and my old pussycat Baby would perch on this little rock down at one end of the island and we'd be yowling at the night lights of Nanaimo." Missing his girlfriend, Ed would drive down to the wharf and blink his headlights on and off, knowing that Pat would be watching.

When they were both 19 years old, Ed and Pat decided to give lightkeeping a try themselves. That was almost four decades ago. Since then the Kidders have gone from being the new kids on the lights to being the wise old owls of lightkeeping. After 28 years at Nootka alone, the couple have had hands-on involvement in 20 lifesaving incidents.

One rescue the Kidder family won't soon forget took place on the night of January 10, 1989, when Pat heard a desperate Mayday over the radio. The caller's English wasn't good, but he seemed to be indicating that a lot of people were in trouble. Ed and his son Dean alerted the Coast Guard and launched the Zodiac. When they reached Descubierto Point, they found a clam boat with its windows closed. Inside were two Coleman stoves, a Coleman heater and a Vietnamese family of six who responded to neither shouts nor shakes. All on board had severe carbon-monoxide poisoning. Ed and Dean got them onto shore where they were revived, but they still had to be evacuated by Canadian Coast Guard helicopter. Kerosene lamps were lit to illuminate the landing site, and local tugboats came in to shine their spotlights on the point of land where the chopper set down.

Another Mayday came over the radio on a cold night in March. Quickly lowering his inflatable into the water, Ed searched for a lost fishing boat halfway down to Escalante Rocks. The *Doughboy* had flipped after striking a deadhead, but three hours later there was still no sign of the boat, and Ed feared he was searching for bodies. When he finally located the vessel, two men were huddled on its overturned hull and another was being kept afloat by a big fish box. The rest were in the water. Until they heard the sound of Ed's boat, the crew of the *Doughboy* thought they were going to die.

Of his many rescues, Ed says simply, "It wasn't a matter of heroics. It was a matter of being human."

Pat and Ed refuse to accept pro-automation arguments that ignore the crucial role light-keepers can play in search-and-rescue operations. Pat expresses her anger with the government's treatment of keepers by waving a riding crop in the faces of any bureaucrats who visit the station. Both suspect the destaffing fight is far from over. "The bureaucrats and politicians are very good at using their lies and statistics," says Pat, "but they can't stop us from fighting tooth and nail for safety on the coast."

Marking the entrance to Nootka Sound, the light-station overlooks Friendly Cove from atop San Rafael Island. In 1929 Emily Carr visited the lighthouse and described it as "a strange wild perch" on a "nosegay of rocks, bunched with trees, spiced with wildflowers."

The lights never go off at Nootka lightstation, which guides vessels along the Vancouver Island coast between Quatsino and Clayoquot Sounds and enables them to seek shelter in Nootka Sound during rough weather.

Aviation Weathers

Ed Kidder measures the dewpoint at the Stevenson screen in preparation for his evening aviation weather report. Nootka is one of 17 stations in British Columbia that provide information specifically for pilots eight times a day. An accurate description of the visibility conditions is especially important for pilots flying between remote coastal communities. Their flight plans aren't filed without checking the keepers' aviation weathers first. Terry Shields, a pilot on British Columbia's coast for 17 years and a representative for the BC Aviation Council, believes that the keepers are an essential safety resource for pilots. "Pretty well all our decisions are based on lighthouse information," he says. "It's as crucial to us as the engine in the plane."

A self-described nighthawk, keeper Pat Kidder spends her nights on the radio making friends with voices. Tired mariners coming down the coast will call her in the wee hours of the morning just to talk. Pat also chats with her fellow keepers on the ALAN radio circuit. Known as the "kelpvine," the system is anything but private. Conversations can be heard by people at the 10 other stations on the circuit and anyone else who happens to own a scanner. Pat has even gone into town and discovered that a grocery clerk knew all the latest details of her personal life.

PART THREE

Northern Lights

The keepers of British Columbia's most northerly lighthouses live, work and endure in some of the province's most hostile environments. Pummelled by storms of awesome power, shrouded in mantles of fog, and caked with frozen spray, the northern lights are lonely outposts of humanity in an awe-inspiring but unforgiving wilderness.

Even for those seeking absolute seclusion, the northern lights sometimes offered more than they bargained for. Madness, suicide and disaster were all too commonplace in the early years. Even in the age of air travel and satellite communications, the North remains a proving ground where extremes of isolation can put the most self-reliant keepers to the test.

Above: Forty-two miles northwest of Cape Scott, the lightstation on Triangle Island commenced operations in 1910 only to be abandoned 10 years later. The tower was intended to serve as a leading light for vessels travelling between Prince Rupert and Vancouver and as a landfall light for trans-Pacific shipping. Perched 198 metres above the water, though, the station's powerful beams were unable to penetrate the almost-constant fog that shrouded the island.

Opposite: *Notice to Mariners #88*, issued by the Dominion of Canada in 1913, quietly announced the Department of Marine and Fisheries' latest achievement in clause 23: "Dixon Entrance—Queen Charlotte Islands—Langara Island—Langara Point—light and fog alarm established."

Top left: Marking the northwestern entrance to Christie Passage, one of the last stretches of sheltered water before northbound ships venture into Queen Charlotte Sound, Scarlett Point lightstation also alerts mariners to extensive below-water rocks and drying ledges that lie nearby. The light first shone in 1905 and has a range of 18 miles.

Bottom left: On the southwest coast of Sarah Island, just north of Klemtu, near Princess Royal Island, Boat Bluff lightstation was erected in 1907 to warn vessels about Hazard Rock in Sarah Passage.

Top right: Established in 1907, Pine Island lighthouse indicates the northwest entrance to Gordon Channel in Queen Charlotte Strait. In 1967 the station was rebuilt at a higher elevation after a 16.7-metre rogue wave wiped out the engine room, fog-alarm building, helicopter pad and practically everything else. Fortunately keeper Pen Brown and his family escaped in time and spent the night outside, huddling around a fire.

Left: Constructed in 1960 in Hecate Strait to warn the increasing marine traffic headed to and from Alcan's new smelter at Kitimat of the reefs, rocks and ledges surrounding it, Bonilla Island station was the last light to be established in British Columbia. Today Bonilla is a favourite among Coast Guard pilots for two reasons: the excellent beachcombing and the famous mud pie made by keeper Harvey Bergen's wife, Nora.

Quatsino

"THE LAST THING YOU EXPECT AT A LIGHTHOUSE IN THE MIDDLE OF NOWHERE IS A KNOCK ON THE DOOR," SAYS QUATSINO KEEPER PAT MICKEY IN A GRUFF VOICE THAT BELIES THE GLEAM IN HIS EYES.

The 58-year-old Albertan pauses in his story to show me how to jig my rod. We are fishing for lingcod in two-metre swells off Kains Island. Pat is telling me about the time he was surprised by an unexpected visitor at the station he worked at the previous year. In the swells he describes as perfect for fishing, I'm trying not to throw up.

Above: Lighthouse life necessitates a close relationship between husband and wife. Pat and Lorraine Mickey are together 24 hours a day. "We're a team," explains Lorraine. "He never gave a second thought about changing a diaper, and I never think twice about pushing a wheelbarrow."

Established in 1907 on Kains Island at the northwestern entrance to Quatsino Sound, Quatsino lighthouse provides the only staffed weather reports between Cape Scott and Nootka. Tugboat captains in particular prefer lightkeepers' reports to the often unreliable information from the automated marine-weather stations on Sartine and Solander Islands off the northwest coast of Vancouver Island. As Pat explains, if you're towing a load, you want firsthand information about sea conditions.

A fierce wind known as a "Qualicum special" was blowing the night Pat's surprise guest showed up. When Pat's wife, Lorraine, woke him in the middle of the night, insisting someone was banging on the door, he thought she was crazy. After all, they were at Sisters Islets lightstation on an isolated rock in the middle of the Strait of Georgia. But he reluctantly headed out to investigate.

"I didn't see or hear anything," he tells me, pulling the gaff out of his lingcod, "but since I was already out there, I thought I might as well take a leak." As he leaned over the railing, he was interrupted by a holler for help. He turned around in shock and found himself staring at a barefoot and hypothermic fisherman whose 3.6-metre-long aluminum boat had been swamped. Briefly dumbfounded, Pat zipped up, took the frantic man inside and alerted the Coast Guard.

After Pat and Lorraine moved to Quatsino, they were cautioned to expect a different kind of knock on their door. Later, over a cod dinner, they tell Chris and me, or "the two pukes" as they affectionately call us, about the infamous "Walter," Kains Island's resident ghost.

The 18-year-old Danish brother-in-law of the lighthouse's first keeper drowned in 1915 while visiting the station. His gravestone, cleared of weeds and surrounded by a freshly painted white picket fence, sits behind the station's third house. Since his death, Walter has developed a reputation for making lights flicker and floorboards creak. Visiting work crews have run from the house near his burial site and refused to return; a former female keeper felt Walter pinch her bottom; and a pilot swore he saw an apparition of an old man lurking around the boathouse. "The thing about ghost stories on the lights is each time you hear them, they just get better and better," Lorraine says. "I haven't seen Walter yet, and I'm sure not expecting him for a visit anytime soon."

Above: There are no safe landing spots on Quatsino Sound's Kains Island. The station boat must be lowered to the water with a highline.

Left: Pat Mickey checks the level of a diesel-fuel tank. It takes 141 litres of fuel a day to run the generators that supply power to everything on the station, from the light in the tower to the microwave oven in Pat's kitchen. Once or twice a year, fuel is pumped from a barge into five 8183-litre tanks.

Assistant keeper Paul Hollyoak examines Quatsino's low-maintenance beacon. A far cry from the awe-inspiring Fresnel lens at Pachena Point, humble lights like this one are the rule rather than the exception at most stations.

Learning on the Lights

The five Hollyoak children are just finishing the last bites of their pancake breakfast when their mother, Audrey, lets out a shout. "I think I see some porpoises out there. No, wait, they're whales...killer whales!"

Darryl, Sean, Hannah, Maya and Gareth hurry outside to get a closer look as the pod of orcas slips into Quatsino Sound.

Although Audrey and Paul Hollyoak sometimes worry that it might be hard for their children to adapt to regular classrooms in the future, they believe lighthouse life has been beneficial as a whole. With Mom as their teacher, the children learn as much from nature's book as the compulsory correspondence lessons. Paul notes that while some children need to be constantly entertained, his are able to invent their own games. With the world of the imagination for a playground, boredom is a foreign concept to them.

Cape Scott

THE DECAYING DRIFTWOOD FENCE THAT MEANDERS ALONG THE SANDNECK AT GUISE BAY IS A REMINDER OF THE COURAGEOUS COMMUNITY THAT TRIED TO TAME THE WILD LANDSCAPE OF CAPE SCOTT IN THE EARLY 1900S.

The reclamation fence was an attempt by Danish pioneer Nels Jensen to convert the sand into pasture for farming. Through such efforts Jensen and the Danish colonists who settled in the area were soon producing butter, jam and beef for market. However, they couldn't overcome the isolation of Vancouver Island's northern tip and eventually abandoned their farms.

Chris and I have just hiked the 24-kilometre trail from San Josef Bay to Guise Bay that the Danish settlers walked after they disembarked from the steamer *Tees* in 1898. Along the way, we passed the remains of their homesteads surrendered to the salal and blackberry canes: a rusted school desk, a leather boot, a wooden wagon wheel, a fallen cedar doorframe. I curse my backpack when I scramble over another windfall, but as Chris reminds me, settlers once hauled everything from groceries to potbellied iron stoves along this trail in weather more miserable than today's. It is hard to imagine families living in this wild rainforest among the bears, cougars and wolves whose fresh tracks in the mud we try to ignore.

The only inhabitants of Cape Scott now are the light-keepers. The lighthouse, originally built in 1959 to aid ship-

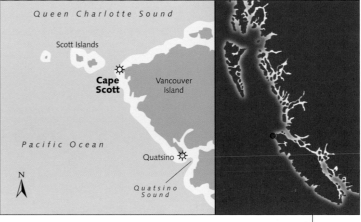

ping traffic in and out of Alcan's new smelter at Kitimat, guides vessels around the northern tip of Vancouver Island. Mariners sometimes call keeper Glenn Borgens to get an early warning of conditions they can expect once they round the tip of the island. When not on duty, Glenn tries to spend as much time as possible exploring the provincial park that surrounds the station. It was on the beach at Experiment Bight that he found his first beachcombing treasure.

On the bottom of the green glass ball is a symbol that looks like an upside-down seven with a stroke through it. In fact, it is a Japanese character meaning "north," indicating that this ball is a fishing float from the Hukuyo Canned Crab Company. The float escaped from its fishing net and travelled more than 5000 miles across the Pacific Ocean before washing up in Cape Scott Provincial Park—intact. It is one of three that Glenn has found during the three weeks he's been at Cape Scott light.

Above: Winter storms often toss treasures like this glass fishing float onto the pristine beaches of Cape Scott Provincial Park.

"The beachcombing here is phenomenal," Glenn tells me. "Low tide is like a Christmas present every day." He has collected a turquoise woven fishing net, an orange US Coast Guard floating electric light, and a laminated business card belonging to one Mr. Young Heung, a man whose advertised services include selling wire, fixing engines and washing laundry in Korea. But Glenn is still seeking the ultimate prize: a perfectly spherical glass float, bigger than a basketball and still encased in its netting.

Japanese glass floats can range from five to 50 centimetres in diameter; are round, cylindrical or pear-shaped; and may be green, blue, purple, pink and gold in colour. According to Amos Woods's book *Beachcombing for Japanese Glass Floats*, lost floats get caught in the Japanese current known as "Kuroshio." They circle around the Pacific Ocean until the right storm pushes them out of the current and onto the West Coast. While most take less than three years to arrive in North America, recently floats dating as far back as 1910 have been discovered. Glenn knew of a lightkeeper who collected more than 100 floats during his 20-year career.

Glenn's good luck and Woods's belief that 14 million floats are still adrift in the North Pacific prompted Chris and me to spend an extra day at Cape Scott Provincial Park so we could search for glass balls. We did find sand dollars, bright plastic floats and the sun-bleached skull of a seal but, alas, despite hours of searching and two very sore necks, no glass balls.

Each year approximately 2000 hikers cross a tenuous suspension bridge to reach Cape Scott's foghorn building at the northernmost tip of Vancouver Island. According to the keepers, the place is a favourite spot for marriage proposals.

In 1959 Cape Scott's four-metre-high light was constructed on the base of an old radar tower, which had been put up by the Royal Canadian Air Force in 1942 after the area was taken over by the military.

Langara Point

IT WAS THE FIRST THING THEY SAW WHEN THEY ARRIVED AND THE LAST THING THEY SPOTTED UPON LEAVING. FOR THE TRANSOCEANIC STEAMERS DESTINED FOR PRINCE RUPERT AT THE TURN OF THE CENTURY, LANGARA LIGHTHOUSE WAS THE FIRST SIGHT OF CANADA.

Established in 1913, the major landfall light that marks Dixon Entrance looks just as striking from the cockpit of the Coast Guard Sikorsky S-61 helicopter as it must have from the port-hole of a steamer. From the air, it is easy to see why this lightstation, which sits on the north-western tip of Langara Island in the Queen Charlotte Islands, is the perfect place from which to observe weather systems from the North Pacific approach the BC coast.

I catch a glimpse of Langara's massive Fresnel lens when the pilots make a tight turn around the tower for the benefit of their extra passengers. In addition to the supplies for Langara, the chopper is carrying six Grade 5 students from Masset Elementary School. Some of the kids acted nonchalant about the flight before takeoff, but all are thrilled now at the sight of the lighthouse standing 48.8 metres above water on the edge of a rocky cliff.

With animated eyes and a ready hug, lightkeeper Judy Schweers introduces herself as we disembark from the helicopter. A former California schoolteacher, Judy came on the lights after a letter-writing courtship with keeper Gordon Schweers. The couple got married at Nootka station on the beaches of Friendly Cove, and their 13-year-old son Guthrie has lived on the lights all his life. After Guthrie shows the kids his menagerie of billy goats, chickens and a tame deer, Judy takes the students up the tower to look at one of only two First Order Fresnel lenses on the BC coast (the other is at Pachena Point).

In 1818, at a mathematics competition sponsored by the French Academy, Augustin Fresnel entered a paper outlining his theory of light diffraction. He won, and thus began the formidable career of the young mathematician from Broglie, France, in the area of optics and light. Fresnel's greatest achievement was his lighthouse lens, perfected in 1822. While a mariner at sea could see only 3.5 percent of the light from an open flame in a tower, Fresnel's new lens allowed him to see 83 percent of that same light. Fresnel's lenses came in several sizes, ranging in height from 43 centimetres for a Sixth Order channel light to three metres for a First Order landfall light.

Above: Langara lighthouse was erected in 1913 on the northwest point of Langara Island, the most northerly of the Queen Charlotte Islands. Isolated as it is, the station receives few visitors. Keeper Judy Schweers gets so wired the night before the Coast Guard chopper's "grocery run" that she can hardly sleep.

Langara's lens is a superlative example of Fresnel's work. It consists of four flash panels, each with a convex glass bull's-eye in its centre that looks like a giant magnifying glass. Concentric rings of catadioptric prisms around the bull's-eye collect, bend and focus all light from a 500-watt bulb into a concentrated horizontal beam. When the lens rotates, the beam is perceived as a flash.

The lens is a hit with the kids, all of whom could easily fit inside the mammoth structure. For one impressed boy, the lens beat out even the helicopter ride as the coolest part of what he described as "the most awesome field trip ever."

Above: Although cleaning the lens is one of 21-year-old assistant keeper Shawn Rose's more basic duties, he also files some of the most complex weather reports on the BC coast. Langara is one of two stations that provides synoptic reports for the World Meteorological Organization (WMO). After Shawn collects data for the standard marine and aviation weather reports, he analyzes the information and converts it into a numerical code. The coded data is in turn used by the WMO to help examine national and international weather patterns and assist in forecasting.

Left: Guthrie Schweers strains to squeeze out a tune on his bagpipes during an impromptu jam session with Shawn Rose.

Previous page: Langara's powerful First Order Fresnel lens has a range of 19 miles, which makes it in an excellent guide for trans-Pacific shipping heading to and from Prince Rupert through Dixon Entrance.

Green Island

The most northern lighthouse in British Columbia is also the windiest. Located one and a half miles east of Dundas Island and 10 miles west of Port Simpson, Green Island lightstation was established in 1906.

The barren island gets the worst of it when the outflow winds blow down Portland Inlet from Alaska and the southeasterlies sweep up Chatham Sound. In the month of December alone, lightkeeper Serge Pare has recorded storm-force winds 12 times. "Up here we get 50- and 60-knot winds not for a day or two but for weeks," he says. "That's when the house starts to crack. The wind is so strong, it blows the paint off."

The winds can pose a serious threat to boats and aircraft in the area. As traffic has increased between Prince Rupert, Port Simpson, Kincolith and villages along the Nass Valley, the keepers' around-the-clock weather reports have become more valuable. Sometimes just getting to the radio room to do the reports can be a challenge. "It's definitely a different kind of life," says Serge, laughing, "usually best for people who are ... well, different."

Serge laughs a lot. He tells me that it is even more important to keep a positive outlook on things when you are living in isolation. On his coffee table are a dictionary full of pressed four-leaf clovers and a worn copy of *How to Live 365 Days a Year*. The Coast Guard's monthly helicopter trip to the island also gives him a boost.

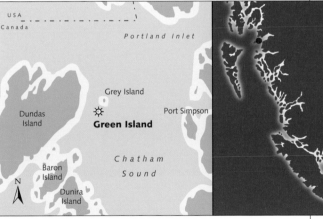

He hums a tune as he digs into the mailbag delivered by chopper along with the groceries and supplies. "Getting food is not so important," he tells me. "What I really look forward to is the mail." Serge organizes his 30 days' worth of mail into piles: one for the overdue bills, one for the out-of-date advertising flyers, one for last month's newspapers and one for his personal correspondence. He pops two chocolate-covered cherries into his mouth—this month's order from Overwaitea included three boxes of Ganong chocolates—and begins to search through his letters.

Then he waves an envelope stamped with red hearts at me. It is a valentine from his girlfriend in Terrace, postmarked only three weeks ago. Instead of ripping it open immediately, Serge puts it away and spreads out last week's *Prince Rupert This Week*. He'll wait for a day when he's feeling down to read the card. He winks at me and says, "Sometimes you have to

Above: Nineteen metres above sea level, Green Island's flashing white light has a range of 13 miles and guides marine traffic between Alaska and Prince Rupert. Only the hardy and resourceful can cope with life in such a remote location.

Previous pages: "They call it Green because it's not." This common saying among keepers reflects Green Island's status as an extremely unpopular station. No trees grow in this harsh, wind-battered landscape. Indeed, the legend of the lightkeeper who kept her children clipped to the clothesline to prevent them from blowing into the sea is well-known along the northern BC coast.

Right: Keeper Serge Pare checks the diesel engines that are the standard source of power for most lightstations. The generators convert diesel fuel into electricity and must be maintained constantly.

Below: Beyond the rocky shores of Green Island rise the mountainous islands of the Alaskan Panhandle. The first users of the station's services were prospectors headed north in search of gold.

save the good stuff. It's letters like these that keep you whistling."

There are many other things Serge has experienced at the lighthouse that make living in such isolation worthwhile: the hundreds of porpoises that were cavorting on both sides of the island when he first arrived by boat, the vivid green and pink light beams of the aurora borealis, the ice sculptures that form around the rocks in the winters. "Just yesterday I saw an eagle swoop down and grab a seagull just like that," he says with a snap of his fingers. "Now that's not something you'd normally see if you've got a regular day job in the city."

Left: Serge Pare drives a tractor full of groceries up to his house. Each month a Coast Guard helicopter drops off his supplies and picks up his next month's shopping list. Although having a personal shopper pick out groceries may sound like a luxury, for many keepers it is a source of frustration. Common complaints include overripe produce, no comparison shopping, and inadequate substitutions. At some lights, deliveries are made by Coast Guard ship. Delays are common, and food may sit in the hold for weeks.

Below left: Serge looks forward to getting news from "the outside world" and the latest video blockbuster in his monthly mail run.

Below right: Serge carved his extra-large oars from driftwood he found on the beach one summer. The original oars of the station boat and everything else in it were washed away in a storm.

Triple Islands

IF A PRINCE RUPERT RESIDENT GETS ANGRY WITH YOU, HE MAY TELL YOU TO GO STRAIGHT TO TRIPLE. THIS ISOLATED STATION IS KNOWN AS "LITTLE ALCATRAZ" OR, AS ONE PATRON OF A LOCAL DRINKING HOLE PUT IT, "A GREAT PLACE TO SEND YOUR ENEMIES, ESPECIALLY IF YOU WANT TO DRIVE THEM CRAZY."

Triple's bad reputation is due to its setting. Situated at the entrance to Brown Passage, the station sits on a rock about the size of a convenience store. The only places to walk on the island are around the helicopter pad, around the roof or up and down the tower. In the winter, keepers are often barricaded indoors as the ocean pounds the walls of their small dwelling.

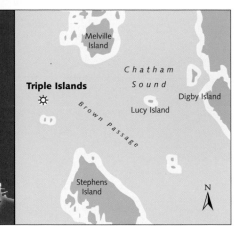

Melville Island

Chatham Sound

Triple Islands
☼

Brown Passage

Digby Island

Lucy Island

Stephens Island

N

Above: With half his life spent at Triple Islands lighthouse and the other half spent on his pink-and-green hand-crafted catamaran, keeper Ed Beard feels uncomfortable on the rare occasions he's away from the ocean.

"There's nowhere to go, nowhere to run and nowhere to hide," says keeper Bill Bemister. "But you know, that doesn't keep me from wanting to come back the minute I leave."

It took several attempts to build what was the first combined concrete lighthouse dwelling and tower in British Columbia. Finally Triple opened for business in 1921. Standing on its rocky outcrop like a medieval fortress, the lightstation helps ships navigate the dangerous passage to Prince Rupert by way of Langara Island.

Triple's keepers work 28 days on, followed by 28 days off. Each month two fly out and two more fly in to the province's only remaining rotational station. Because of its cramped living quarters and its lack of open spaces, Triple was ultimately designated a bachelor station. Even so, it can be a strain for two men to live in such close proximity to each other for a month. Sometimes a practical joke can ease the tension. Once, Bill awoke to find a pair of glazed-over petrel eyes staring straight at him. His partner, keeper Ed Beard, had found the dead bird on the catwalk of the lantern room and placed it on the stairs to surprise Bill. "That sure woke me up all right!" says Bill with a laugh and a sidelong glance at Ed.

Both men admit that life on Triple can be stressful. Bill tells me that there have been cases of insanity, suicide and "more attempted murders than anyone's ever known about" at the station. One keeper left a tattered note under a mattress claiming his partner was trying to kill him. Another went mad and smashed in his own head with a sledgehammer. His partner bandaged him up and alerted the RCMP, but a gale prevented anyone from getting to the island for four more days. By that time the man had ripped off his bandages and shot himself in the head. Such stories only serve to amplify Triple's notoriety in Prince Rupert.

Previous page: Rising impressively out of the wild seas of Brown Passage, Triple helped to open up a northern approach to Prince Rupert.

Top: Playfully mocking the cliché of the old-time lightkeeper scanning the sea for signs of trouble, assistant keeper Bill Bemister fools around with his antique spyglass.
Bottom: Triple Islands light is a difficult posting at the best of times. In 1979 an engineer was killed when a freak wave swept him off the rocks on which he stood.
Right: Over the roar of a Sikorsky S-61 helicopter, relief keeper Shawn Rose shouts out a greeting after quickly unloading his gear on Triple.

Dryad Point

AFTER FIVE DAYS OF RAIN DRUMMING THE ROOF OF OUR VAN, TWO ABORTED HELICOPTER TAKEOFFS AND ONE DESTRUCTIVE STORM THAT SENT FIVE-METRE WATERSPOUTS SKITTERING ACROSS PRINCE RUPERT'S HARBOUR, CHRIS AND I FINALLY MAKE IT TO DRYAD POINT LIGHTSTATION, ESTABLISHED NEAR BELLA BELLA IN 1899.

We are greeted with a rainbow over the tower. "You guys must have good luck," keeper Frank Dwyer says as we climb out of the chopper. "We've had mostly rain, rain, rain this winter. But you know, we're never sure what the weather will do next out here."

When Frank first took the job as lightkeeper, he wasn't sure what to expect. "I probably had the same romantic ideas as most people do," he says as we walk toward the radio room. "You know, sitting up in the tower on stormy nights, ready to jump into a little rowboat in 10-foot seas to save people." He laughs. "That's not exactly how it works."

In fact, the majority of his work is preventative. Frank's up-to-the-minute and accurate reports describing conditions at the junction of Lama Passage and Seaforth Channel are essential to mariners and pilots planning their routes along the Inside Passage.

"So, what's the weather like today?" Frank asks his five-year-old son Connor.

Connor pulls his Teenage Mutant Ninja Turtle toque down over his ears and looks up at the sky before passing judgement. "Overcast," he says with certainty, "with a little bit of blue sky."

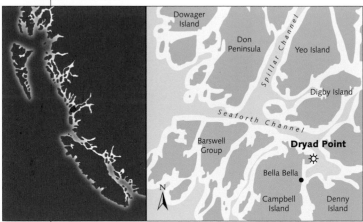

Above: *Connor and Carrie Dwyer make a quick exit from Dryad Point's 7.3-metre tower as the foghorn begins to sound.*

Frank turns to me with the smile of a proud father. Being able to spend time with his three children is one of the things he enjoys most about his job. He also likes teaching them about the weather. "Now Connor and I will show you how we find the ceiling for aviation weathers," he says to me, and hands his son a large red helium-filled balloon.

Frank explains that the height at which 60 percent of the sky is covered with clouds is the ceiling. This height is the maximum altitude from which the earth is visible, something that pilots need to know before they take off. When Connor releases the balloon, they will time how long it takes for it to disappear into the clouds. The balloon, issued by Canada's Atmospheric Environment Service, rises at a rate of 140 metres per minute.

We all count to three and Connor lets go. The red balloon rises past the white tower and into the sky. Connor looks expectantly at his father when it starts to disappear.

"Four minutes and five seconds," Frank says, "An 1878-foot ceiling."

"See?" Connor says to me with a grin. "It's easy!".

It's not the first meteorology lesson I've received from Dryad Point's five-year-old weather wizard. Upon our arrival, Connor politely corrected me when I commented on the stormy weather. "It's not storming out," he said. "It's raining." Then he added seriously, "There's a big difference."

Above: As his father looks on, Connor Dwyer prepares to release the helium-filled balloon that they will use to measure the ceiling—the maximum height from which the earth is visible—for Dryad lightstation's aviation weather report.

Left: A Sikorsky S-61 heads toward Dryad Point lightstation. The "workhorse of the North" can haul 3375 kilograms and up to 23 passengers.

Following pages: Dryad Point lighthouse sits at the junction of Lama Passage and Seaforth Channel. At 11.6 metres above sea level, its occulting white and red lights warn mariners of foul ground near the point and around nearby islands and guide vessels bound to or from Bella Bella.

PART FOUR

Beacons of the Inside Passage

lthough the waters of the Inside Passage are sheltered, they can be deceptively dangerous. The labyrinth of islets and islands in the passage that stretches from Vancouver to Prince Rupert is swept by impetuous tides and studded with unseen reefs. Place names like Tide Rip Passage, Terror Point, Mantrap Inlet, Choked Passage, Mystery Reef, Danger Shoal, Devils Hole and Whirlpool Rapids reflect the wariness with which these waters were regarded by early mariners. Until 1898 there were no lights north of Chrome Island on the Inside Passage and traffic passing that way was confined to travel in the daylight hours.

Gold fever changed everything. The thousands of people bound for the Klondike when gold was discovered in 1897 travelled mostly by ship. The resulting surge of traffic, abetted by the emergence of salmon canneries, pulp mills and construction of a rail terminus at Prince Rupert in 1906, spurred the building of more than 20 lights marking the Inside Passage between Victoria and Prince Rupert during the next 10 years.

Above: Saturna Island lightstation began operation in 1888. Located at East Point on the island at the junction of the Strait of Georgia and Boundary Pass, the station indicates the northeastern entrance to the pass and warns mariners of nearby Boiling Reef.

Opposite: The tower at Pulteney Point sits on a gravel spit at the southwest extremity of Malcolm Island in Queen Charlotte Strait. Killer whales sometimes visit to rub themselves on the pebble beaches surrounding the station.

Following pages: Porlier Pass, a narrow channel separating Galiano and Valdes Islands, is swept by strong tidal currents of up to nine knots. This range light, which marks Race Point on the northern tip of Galiano Island, was torn down and replaced by a fibreglass tower in February 1996. The station was destaffed soon after.

Pulteney Point

"I WAS MOWING THE LAWN WHEN I HEARD SOMEONE

DOWN AT THE POINT YELLING, 'HELP, HELP!'" SAYS LIGHTKEEPER TED ASHE.

"I LOOKED OVER AND I COULDN'T STOP LAUGHING."

Ted's tale is a different kind of rescue story. Although it took the strength of four men to carry out the rescue, the victim still ended up dead. The remains are probably still sitting in someone's basement freezer.

The incident took place at Pulteney Point lightstation. Located on the southwestern extremity of Malcolm Island in Queen Charlotte Strait, the light began operation in 1905 and marks an important junction between the broad expanse of Queen Charlotte Strait and the narrower confines of Broughton Strait.

It was a 135-kilogram halibut that Ted saved that day. The cries for help he heard were from an American tourist in a small skiff struggling to bring in the biggest catch of his life. "This was a barn door. We're talking 300 pounds," says Ted. "And all this guy had was a jig."

The halibut was impossible to control, so Ted shot it with his .22. There remained the big problem of getting the fish into the tourist's boat. It was physically impossible for a single person to do it, so the three-man crew that was working at the station came out to help. "We literally had to drag that thing up the beach," recalls Ted. "Then we pulled the nose to the tail and all four of us took it down to the boat."

Although the tourist's boat was already low in the water with the three other (much smaller) halibut he had caught that day, he didn't offer to share with men who had spent more than an hour saving his fish. "Nope," says Ted with a shake of his head. "He just got in his boat full of fish and puttered off."

Above: Sixteen-year-old Lynae Ashe completes a flip on the trampoline in her backyard. Unlike most lighthouse kids, Lynae and her siblings attend public school. Keeper Ted Ashe's posting at Pulteney Point allows him and his family to interact with the local community.

Colin Ashe heads for the beach as the late-afternoon light casts shadows on Pulteney station.

Below: Established in 1905, the flashing red and white lights at Pulteney Point lighthouse indicate the separation of Broughton and Queen Charlotte Straits and guide mariners bound north and south.

Top left: "They call it a one-man station, but we call it a family station," says keeper Karen Ashe, referring to the absence of an assistant keeper at Pulteney Point. Whenever they can, the Ashes' children—Shayla, Lynae and Colin—help them run the station smoothly.

Top right: The station's helicopter pad is a favourite play spot for Colin and Shayla.

Perils of the Deep

Pulteney Point lighthouse was the scene of an unforgettable experience in May 1922. Two men, Cook and Philip, were waiting for the lighthouse tender one morning when they saw what they assumed was a ship's mast rising above the rough seas. As the object came closer, they realized with a shock that it was a strange creature with its head and neck out of the water. Cook's sketch depicts an animal with a long, rounded body, an extended neck, a small head and an enormous eye. He estimated it to be 7.6 metres long but only 30 centimetres wide and described it as having "brown scaly skin and large filmy eyes similar to those of a cow." When it travelled through the water, it moved its long neck back and forth like a snake. According to Paul LeBlond and Edward Bousfield's book *Cadborosaurus: Survivor from the Deep*, the Pulteney experience is similar to many other sea-creature sightings reported along the coast over the years.

Cape Mudge

STANDING ON THE FERRY FROM CAMPBELL RIVER TO QUADRA ISLAND
EN ROUTE TO THE CAPE MUDGE LIGHTHOUSE, I WATCH THE SEA LIONS RELAX
ON THEIR BACKS AS THE TIDE TAKES THEM FOR A RIDE UP THE CHANNEL
AT A RATE OF SEVEN TO NINE KNOTS.

In exploring the shores of Cape Mudge, Chris and I are following the path of none other than Captain George Vancouver. On July 13, 1792, Vancouver anchored HMS *Discovery* and *Chatham* in the southern entrance to the passage and rowed ashore to meet the First Nations peoples who had lived on the cape for thousands of years. Vancouver named the cape after Zachary Mudge, his 22-year-old first lieutenant.

It was one of the earliest contacts between Europeans and the peoples of the Kwakwaka'wakw nation. However, it would be another 100 years before gold fever brought the white man to the south end of Quadra Island on a permanent basis. In 1898 a lighthouse was established at Cape Mudge to mark the entrance to Discovery Passage and warn the flow of vessels heading up to the Klondike of the marine dangers in the area.

Strong tidal currents can generate large standing waves at Cape Mudge; wild seas can be created when a strong southeast wind opposes a flooding tide. The racing water and dangerous shoals around the cape have spelled the end of many small vessels and some not so small. It is the lightkeepers who are often the first to notice mariners in

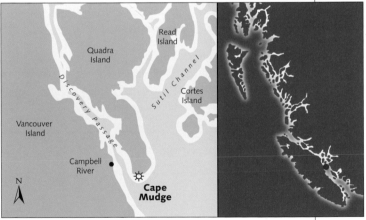

trouble and the first to alert help. Even so, the Cape Mudge lightstation has been equipped by the Coast Guard with technology designed to replace lightkeepers.

When keeper Dennis Johnston shows me the rows of solar-powered batteries inside the aluminum box beside the tower, an alarm buzzes in a Comox office. Dennis gets a phone call and assures the caller that it is really him, not vandals or thieves. At the lightstation is an estimated $100,000 automated weather-observing system in addition to a solar-powered light, horn and videograph fog sensor.

While Dennis is anything but a technophobe and supports changes that can save the taxpayer money and reduce harm to the environment, he is skeptical about the present equipment's ability to replace the services that Cape Mudge keepers have offered since the light was first established. "Technology can help us, but it can't take our place," he says. "I certainly don't think that it can work as well as we have for the past 100 years."

Above: Cape Mudge keeper Dennis Johnston holds on to the new solar-powered foghorns. Prompted by a videograph sensor that reads the moisture in the air automated horns have proven one of the Coast Guard's less reliable innovations.

Left: Cape Mudge lighthouse marks the southern end of Discovery Passage, a busy shipping channel separating Quadra Island from Vancouver Island. Entering the passage is a tug bound for Alaska, towing a barge piled high with everything from automobiles to shipping containers.
Below: A fishing boat bound for the Strait of Georgia heads past the cape.
Bottom: While lighthouses were traditionally designed to adorn the natural beauty of their settings, modern navigational aids like this aluminum shed housing automation equipment seem deliberately contrived to spoil the view.

Chrome Island

KELLY LEWIS SPREADS HIS ARMS WIDE AND LEANS FORWARD AS IF PREPARING FOR AN OLYMPIC HIGH DIVE.

The assistant keeper at Chrome Island lighthouse is giving me a demonstration of the "wind surfing" that he suspects is depicted in the petroglyphs on the island. "The wind blows up this cliff fast and hard," he says of the rock face on which many of the petroglyphs are carved. "I think maybe the Indians were playing on the wind, maybe worshipping it."

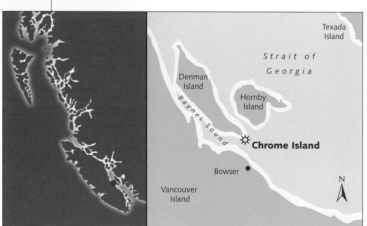

Above: Chrome Island is noted for its great variety of Native petroglyphs.

Chrome Island is located in the northwest corner of the Strait of Georgia. The lighthouse sits 22 metres above the water on the southeast side of the islet and marks the entrance to Baynes Sound. This spot has a special feature: into its sandstone cliffs—once known as Yellow Rock because they glow golden in the setting sun—a series of strange curved shapes and figures are carved.

Kelly's interpretation of the petroglyphs' significance is one of many. Some scholars believe they record the battles of the Puntledge Band Natives who at one time made nearby Denman Island their summer home. Others suggest that they have great religious significance, perhaps depicting offerings made to spirit gods.

In fact, very little is understood about Chrome's petroglyphs. Even their age remains unknown. Coming from the Greek word *petra*, meaning "rock," and *glyphe*, meaning "carving," petroglyphs are impossible to date. The ones on Chrome Island may be several hundred, or thousand, years old.

But ever since the lighthouse went up in 1891, they have kept keepers, and visitors like me, forever speculating. One smiling figure that caught my imagination seemed to be holding a fish. Or was it a spear? Maybe I was looking at an ancient lightkeeper waving his flaming torch to signal canoes in the waters. Whatever the figure represented, at one time, people sat on this same rock, heard the same groaning of the sea lions, watched the same moon rise in the sky, and decided to make their mark. As head keeper Barry Shaw put it, "You just can't help but wonder. It may be graffiti. It may be the story of their lives."

Left: Despite his 22 years as a keeper, Barry Shaw is now so fed up with living on a tiny island that he can't wait to retire. "I'm just biding my time till I can get out of here," he says.

Below: Don't leave home without it. Every lightkeeper's essential equipment: gumboots, rain gear, binoculars and a VHF radio.

Above: Assistant keeper Kelly Lewis zooms back to Chrome after returning a movie to Deep Bay. The town is only a mile and a half from the island, making Chrome seem like the perfect compromise between lighthouse solitude and city convenience.

Following pages: The 1500-metre-high peaks of Vancouver Island's Beaufort Range tower above Chrome Island, which lies off the southeastern tip of Denman Island.

Ballenas Islands

AS THE SUN BEGINS TO SET OVER VANCOUVER ISLAND, CHRIS AND I

ENJOY A GLASS OF HOMEMADE BLACKBERRY WINE WITH LIGHTKEEPERS

RICHARD AND RETA WOOD ON THE ISLAND THAT IS THEIR BACKYARD.

Established in 1900, Ballenas Islands lightstation is located in the central-northwest sector of the strait. The light is a long-range visual aid for mariners transiting the wide and deep waterway that Richard assures me can be dangerous nevertheless.

The islands were named *Islas de las Ballenas* or Islands of the Whales by the Spanish explorer Lieutenant Francisco de Eliza after he spotted whales offshore in 1791. Knowing the terrors later sailors experienced travelling these waters, one can scarcely imagine the hardships faced by the crews of the earliest European ships like Eliza's *San Carlos* and *Saturnina*. Not only were there no lighthouses to set courses by, there were not even any charts to follow. Mapmaking was a primary job of the first European explorers. They survived only by proceeding with the utmost caution, moving the larger ships in daylight after the way ahead had been probed by men tirelessly rowing out and back in longboats. Their most useful navigational aid in these inshore waters was probably the leadline, a measured, weighted line that was dropped overboard and laboriously pulled back aboard hundreds of times a day to detect approaching shoals and record depths for the survey.

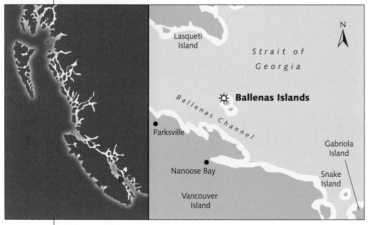

Above: The Strait of Georgia and the Coast Mountains form a perfect backdrop as dawn breaks at Ballenas Islands station. Situated just south of Lasqueti Island, and near Parksville on Vancouver Island, the station's light has a range of 17 miles.

Today anyone wishing to explore the strait may use a detailed chart system and a full range of navigational aids, including electronic chart displays and global positioning systems. But mariners still confirm their positions with the lights. Richard tells me that all the gadgets in the world can't replace the eyes and ears of a human. "The lights link together and provide a safety net for people," he says. "Altogether they represent something really important."

After living at places as remote as Estevan Point, Richard and Reta find that living at Ballenas is a treat. Richard often sees recreational boaters and cruise ships passing by, and it takes him only 20 minutes by boat to get to nearby Parksville on Vancouver Island to do his shopping. "In the old days, keepers would go nuts all alone on this rock in the middle of nowhere," he says. "But today Ballenas is a breeze—an old man's station, really."

When the station first opened, it was considered very isolated. Ballenas's initial keeper, William Brown, went insane while working at the lighthouse. In 1905 his wife, Maggie, tended the light while her husband sat in the Nanaimo jail after being declared a risk to himself and to others by the police. A month later he was back on the lights, but in April 1906, a telegram to the marine agent for the Department of Marine and Fisheries arrived stating: "Lightkeeper Ballenas wants you send immediate relief, apparently insane." Brown was locked away for the rest of his days.

For Richard and Reta, it is society that drives them crazy, not isolation. Isolation offers freedom from driving in traffic each morning, from punching a clock every day, from having your boss breathing down your neck. The couple cherish their solitude. "First thing everyone asks us is: How can you live all alone out here? Who do you talk to?" Richard says, then chuckles. "Who do we talk to? We talk to each other."

"And sometimes ourselves," Reta adds.

"Anyway, Reta and I, we're a couple of reclusives and hedonists out here. So this is exactly our lifestyle." Richard winks at his wife. "And if we want to get a little bit crazy, there's no one to wag their fingers at us."

Richard and Reta Wood enjoy one of their last sunsets on the island. On September 1, 1996, Ballenas was destaffed and the keepers were transferred to Cape Scott.

Above and left: Richard Wood and his Airedale terrier Zelda are constant companions. "On the lights, we spend so much time with our pets that they become just like us," Richard explains. Pets have always been an intrinsic part of lighthouse life. In fact, the first Canadian dog to receive a medal for bravery was Bill the Collie, a lighthouse canine. On August 31, 1927, Cape Beale lightkeeper Philip Cox was awakened at 3:00 a.m. by his pet's barking. The dog dragged his master out of bed just in time; the crew of the *Seawolf* was pulled to safety minutes before the boat was dashed upon the rocks.

Previous pages: The sun rises over Ballenas's 8.2-metre tower. Because most West Coast lighthouses were built on promontories, tall structures weren't necessary for the light to be visible at a distance. Despite its short tower, Ballenas's light shines 21.3 metres above the water.

Merry Island

I AM WONDERING HOW A LIGHTHOUSE KID WHO SPENT MOST OF HIS CHILDHOOD IN ISOLATION GROWS UP TO BE A TEENAGER WHO SPENDS MOST OF HIS FREE TIME IN FRONT OF A CROWD. RIGHT NOW, 17-YEAR-OLD ADAM RICHARDS CAN'T EXPLAIN IT TO ME.

He's at a rehearsal for a high school theatre production. In the weeks to come, he will juggle applying for university, writing his speech for graduation and performing with an improvisational drama troupe. Adam's parents, Don and Kathy, aren't quite sure how it all happened, either.

"For a lighthouse kid, he's quite the extrovert," says lightkeeper Don Richards of his son's love of acting. "Not like me. I'm almost afraid to be in the audience."

Upon his return to the lighthouse, Adam tells me that he doesn't give much credit to prevailing lighthouse stereotypes. "It's true isolation can give you the freedom to be weird," he says, "but it also gives you the freedom to learn new things, learn a hobby and learn about yourself. You can develop a personality instead of a neurosis."

Adam lives at Merry Island lightstation, the only one on the Sunshine Coast. Located in the Strait of Georgia, the light marks the southern entrance to Welcome Pass, separating it from Malaspina Strait. When the station was established in 1903, these two major waterways were crucial to the development of Vancouver's commercial shipping industry; today they also serve growing numbers of pleasure boaters.

Above: A Coast Guard MBB 105 helicopter takes off from the flight deck of the CCGS *Sir Wilfrid Laurier.*

The island is only a short boat ride from the town of Halfmoon Bay. Because civilization is so near, mariners sometimes don't take the same precautions they might if they were farther from shore. Don occasionally helps pleasure boaters who have flooded their engines, run out of fuel or had other mechanical trouble, problems that may not be immediately life-threatening but can easily become dangerous if sea conditions change.

The Richardses have experienced firsthand how quickly the weather can blow up during the 12-minute ride across Welcome Pass. "One time it was blowing 30 [knots] when we left and 50 in the middle," Kathy recalls. "The waves were so big, they were falling over one another and all we could see was water above us. My knees turned to rubber as soon as I got off the boat."

"It's my crystal ball," says Don Richards of the sunshine recorder provided by the Atmospheric Environment Service. The glass sphere magnifies the light from the sun onto graph paper. The burnt paper indicates how many hours of sunshine the Sunshine Coast receives each day.

Kathy prefers to stay on land when possible, but Don and Adam make the trip five days a week so Adam can go to school in town. Over the years they have encountered sea lions, a whale and some very big waves. But only winds more than 40 knots will stop them from crossing, and Adam seldom misses more than 10 days of school a year. The rewards of mingling with classmates and contributing to his community are well worth the bumpy ride and wet clothes of the daily commute.

Still, Adam admits that living at a lighthouse can be a little different. Like the time he showed a group of elementary school children around the lightstation. "I remember thinking, This is kind of weird. I'm taking kids on a field trip to my own home." Nevertheless, he proved to be an entertaining tour guide. "I scared them pretty badly," he says with a grin. "When they least expected it, I blasted the foghorn." Always a true crowd-pleaser.

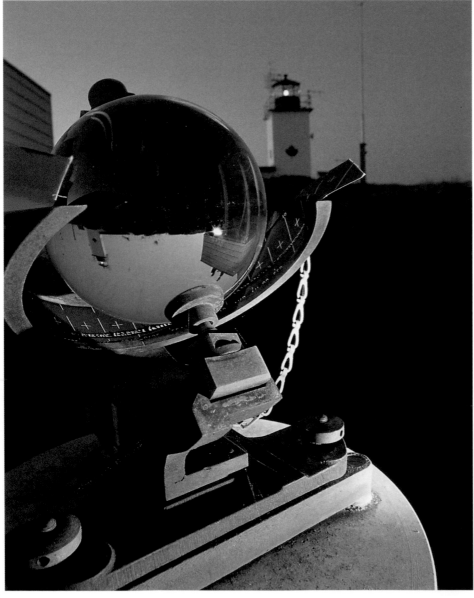

Left: The daily commute: sea spray splashes the windshield of the Richardses' Lifetimer as son Adam takes a turn at the wheel. Once they reach the government dock at Halfmoon Bay, Don and Adam tie up the boat and head down Highway 101 to Chatelech high school in Sechelt.
Below: The CCGS *Sir Wilfrid Laurier* sits in Welcome Pass off Merry Island. The 83-metre light-duty icebreaker's main duties include resupplying lighthouses, tending navigational aids, search-and-rescue, and fisheries enforcement.

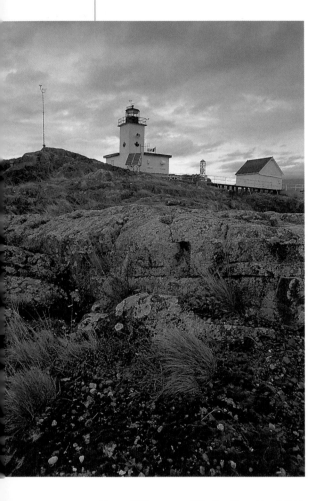

Above: With a range of 16 miles, Merry Island's light indicates the entrance to Welcome Pass and warns mariners of the shoal east of the island.

Right: A crew member from CCGS *Sir Wilfrid Laurier* transports a massive Terra Tank of desalinated water to Merry Island station by open workboat. Although rainwater is collected from the roof and stored in a cistern beneath the keeper's dwelling, this reservoir usually runs out by early spring.

Looking Back

For centuries the gleam of the lighthouse has reassured mariners in the pitch-black of night. Dryad Point's tower, like all guiding lights, signifies safety and sanctuary.

Each time Chris and I drive across Lions Gate Bridge in Vancouver and see the flash from Point Atkinson, we remember the lights we visited and the keepers we met. We imagine Norbie Brand waking up at 3:00 a.m. to report the weather at Cape Beale, Iain Colquhoun heading down the trail from Pachena Point to look for a late hiker, and Pat Kidder chatting to a tugboat captain on the Nootka radiophone. We recall the awe we felt watching Pachena's powerful First Order Fresnel lens slice through the night and the thrill of standing beneath Estevan's cathedral-like flying buttresses. But as we rejoice at British Columbia's good fortune in possessing some of the world's most impressive working lighthouses, we can't help wondering how long all this will be so.

Keepers remained on 27 BC lights when Minister of Fisheries and Oceans David Anderson called a halt to destaffing in 1998, but even then he refused to concede that keepers are needed for reasons of marine safety. At the same time, dismantling of the lighthouse system's rich architectural heritage creeps forward. Point Atkinson, one of only three BC lights accorded national heritage status, has been stripped of many original fittings. The crystal masterpiece in Pachena's lantern room has been turned off, replaced by a standard plastic lamp that sits atop a steel pole outside the tower, and the Coast Guard is now deciding whether or not to remove the Fresnel lens from this recognized heritage building. The official attitude that has resulted in the century-old stone keeper's residence at Race Rocks and other classic edifices being demolished, often to make way for fibreglass and aluminum eyesores, fails to recognize that in a country as young as Canada, lighthouse structures dating back a hundred years and more are among the most historic buildings we possess.

It is time those in charge accepted what the public has been trying to tell them for three decades: that British Columbia's lighthouses are far more than mere traffic lights. They are reminders of the province's rich maritime heritage and monuments to the people who have lived and worked in them since 1860. They are also symbols of hope, for mariners who take comfort in the knowledge friendly eyes watch over them on the most perilous stretches of the coast, and for city dwellers who fuel their dreams by gazing out their windows at the flash across the water.

Acknowledgements

We will never forget the generosity and hospitality of all the lightkeepers who let two strangers toting a notebook and a mountain of camera gear into their lives. Our sincere appreciation goes out to everyone else who made this book possible, including the Canadian Coast Guard and all the people at Harbour Publishing. A special thanks goes to our families for their love and support.

Our visits to Nootka and Estevan Point could not have happened without the transportation provided by Air Nootka in Gold River, British Columbia. To visit these lights, contact Grant Howatt at (250) 283-2255.

Much of the aerial photography in the book was accomplished with the assistance of Sechelt-Gibsons Air. A great pilot is everything when shooting aerials; thanks to Dave Toher for going beyond the call of duty. Those wishing to take a "flight-seeing" tour of British Columbia's lighthouses should contact the airline at 1-800-745-8899 or (604) 885-1062.

Notes on Photography

Most of the images in this book were made with Canon 35 mm equipment. Chris's Canon EOS A2 and EOS 10s camera bodies have withstood a variety of tortures such as being smashed on the rocks, sprayed by salt water and accidentally submerged in fresh water. By the time we finished work on this book, much of Chris's equipment was held together by duct tape and Krazy Glue graciously provided by lightkeepers along the way. Lenses used range in focal lengths from 20 mm to 600 mm. Occasionally a medium-format Mamiya 645 was used for landscape work. A Manfrotto 055C tripod with an Arca Swiss Monoball was employed whenever practical to assist in composition and improve image sharpness.

Film stocks varied according to subject matter and lighting conditions. For images of the towers and landscapes, Fuji Velvia was used for its saturated colour and fine grain. For people and wildlife, Chris often shot Fuji Provia 100 and occasionally Kodak Ektachrome E100SW, while Kodak Ektachrome E200 helped capture action under heavily overcast skies.

Photography Credits

Pg. 28 Vancouver Public Library 2953; pg. 40 & 73 David Nunuk; pg. 63 Ian McAllister; pg. 64 bottom left Chris Mills; & pg. 82 bottom left Buzz Walker.

Harbour Publishing,
PO Box 219,
Madeira Park, BC V0N 2H0

Jacket design, maps, page design and composition by Roger Handling, Terra Firma Digital Arts.
Illustration, P. 1, by Graham Kennell. Illustrations P. 10, 32, 62, 88, by Kim LaFave.

Harbour Publishing acknowledges the financial support of the Government of Canada through the Book Publishing Industry Development Program and the Province of British Columbia through the British Columbia Arts Council, for its publishing activities.

THE CANADA COUNCIL | LE CONSEIL DES ARTS
FOR THE ARTS | DU CANADA
SINCE 1957 | DEPUIS 1957

Printed in Canada

Canadian Cataloguing in Publication Data

Jaksa, Chris, 1971-
  Guiding lights

  Includes index.
  ISBN 1-55017-186-0

  1. Lighthouses—British Columbia—History. 2. Lighthouse keepers— British Columbia—Anecdotes.
3. Lighthouses—British Columbia—Pictorial works. 4. Pacific coast (B.C.)—History.
I. Tanod, Lynn, 1972- II. Title.
VK1027.B7J34 1998   387.1'55'09711   C98-910678-0